Tales of the Abnormalities

Untold True Stories of Police Agencies with Paranormal Activity and Strange Oddities

Larry Larman

PAGE PUBLISHING
Conneaut Lake, PA

First originally published by Page Publishing 2023

The following stories are based on facts resulting from my actual encounters with paranormal and violent situations during my employment with the Maryland National Capital Park and Planning Commission (MNCPPC) and the Office of the Sheriff, Prince George's County, Maryland.

ISBN 979-8-88793-902-5 (pbk)
ISBN 979-8-88793-916-2 (digital)

Printed in the United States of America

CONTENTS

ACKNOWLEDGMENTS

Gina Larman, my wife, for always supporting and being there for me.

Christina Cheek and MaryAnne Leginus, for their unrelenting help and tireless devotion to the completion of this book.

To my earlier employer, the Maryland National Capital Park and Planning Commission (MNCPPC), and all the surrounding law enforcement agencies.

INTRODUCTION

I am not a historian. I am writing my own personal life experience based on vivid recollections burned into my memory, especially as a member of the law enforcement community. I am also including a portion of my own personal history, which I hope will give you some perspective about me.

You may find some of the episodes or incidents I describe as a police officer to be incredible or unbelievable. While I do not have video or audio to verify any of them, I assure you they are true. I know other officers who have witnessed unusual phenomena, like what I will describe for you. They will not come forward with experiences out of concern that their stories will be discredited as untruthful or exaggerated.

I understand the reader may be skeptical about the stories I am going to share. I would probably be a skeptic, too, if not for my share of sightings, sounds, and confrontations when I wasn't sure of what was really happening or what I was seeing.

I had many of these experiences working as a police officer, not as a ghost hunter. Like any investigator, I can explain with a reasonable degree of assurance the *who, what, when, where,* and *why* of many of these episodes. But there is more to each story. We as living beings do not exist alone. There are substances, like bad shadows or dark residues, which also occupy our space and time, in places where bad things have happened. People walked this earth before us, releasing and leaving behind both positive and negative energy, and now it's our turn. We will leave residue as well.

In most of the incidents described in this book, I will be focusing on the negative energy and the dark residue at locations throughout the State of Maryland's Prince George's County. Some, if not nearly all, the county park system's open areas have had deaths occur in them, and some parks more than others. Accidental or natural deaths, murders, suicides, and murder-suicides have all occurred within the park system. Shootings, stabbings, beatings…you name it, it has happened. Incidents like these do not just occur in cities. They happen everywhere and are not restricted to one place or one time. Sexual crimes constantly happen within the system due to isolation of the victims within a dark park. I always tell people to stay in populated areas where they will be seen to avoid becoming a victim of these types of crimes.

The Maryland Park Police are aware of problem areas and have always assigned appropriate resources to these areas, including a mounted unit and motorcycle and, foot patrols, as necessary. The current commander of Prince George's County Division, Chief Stanley Johnson, applies saturation techniques to patrol problem parks and prevent or eliminate problem situations effectively. The Maryland Park Police have always acted as a complete unit within the entire park system, including the Montgomery County Division. It is good to know there is a police system within the M-NCPPC that is a very effective unit.

Ghosts or shadows of what did exist, also known as residual hauntings, appeared to me by chance. A residual haunting or effect is not a ghost but energy left behind from a traumatic event. Buildings and locations can absorb this energy, which can replay repeatedly. The entities I encountered were people going about their daily business at the time they were accidentally killed or murdered and left within old buildings or mansions without receiving proper rites. The crimes left behind residual effects of events from the past.

There have been instances of instantaneous death, where people were killed but maintained their performance, unaware they were dead. These types of incidents have occurred in actual military battles. Mathew Brady Studios has a photograph of a Civil War soldier with musket still in hand, charging forward, looking straight ahead, not knowing he was dead. Dying quickly is much preferred to long, drawn-out suffering, such as can happen with disease or critical battle wounds which will not heal or being maimed so badly the person cannot function in their own in life.

The other side of the coin is knowing exactly what is going to happen to you and being unable to do anything about it, such as happens with drowning. In that case, the only thing to do is pray, if you have time.

I have discovered not all entities are shadows or light. Some are outlines of what did exist. Even Julius Caesar complained of ghosts within his palace. Not to be blasphemous, but Jesus Christ reappeared after death to his apostles, as reported in the Gospel. What I have experienced is something most people do not. I was in the field, exposed to these situations, not expecting to encounter what I did, but I would not trade my personal experiences for anything. I do not intend for this book to sound like religious writings, though my experiences have enlightened me to something beyond our physical being. Remember these words: "Father, Son, and Holy Ghost." I personally believe in these words and the animism of it all.

The leftover residue I have encountered and shared in these stories is meant to enlighten people and society about the existence of hidden energy and entities. Most of us are unaware of what is happening around us as these unusual experiences are not shared with us. This information is not being shared or intentionally blocked from becoming public knowledge.

Some of my stories within my personal life and career are very harsh, but as in any policeman's career, it is that way. The other incidents within this book are accounts of murders, perverts, rapists, and absolute criminals. Included within are oddities such as "The Pastor" and "The Spider" that, although not of a serious nature, were very odd situations that occurred to me and to others. The only difference is the spider was alive. It was found to be extremely dangerous due to its predatory nature, immense size, and its location within a nature center visited by small children.

CHAPTER 1

Personal History

My first memory of anything was a very disturbing scene. I had no idea what was happening, only that I had been awakened by screams and violence. With wide-open eyes, I became frightened to the bone as I watched the scene in front of me. I saw, within a corral, a large fire and a fifty-five-gallon drum filled with boiling water, smoke, and steam emanating from it. Men were tying screaming hogs by their feet, lifting them with a makeshift crane, slashing their throats with a large knife, shooting them in the head and lowering them, while still alive, into the drum of boiling water. The hogs thrashed violently, spilling the water onto the flame, almost dousing it. I stood there watching as these animals, one by one, suffered the same ending. I became so frightened, thinking I would be next, that I disobeyed my father's order to stand there and not move. I started to run.

My father chased me, asking, "Where are you going, boy? This is not going to happen to you." He began talking to me, gently soothing my anxiety. Then reality set in. We were farmers, and the hogs were one of our food sources. I continued to watch this slaughter, the stripping of their skins, cutting them open, and contents spilling onto the ground. The smell of blood permeated in the air. I was watching this while being held in my father's arms. It was a disgusting necessity to understand farm procedures and life. It was not easy watching these animals have their throats cut. Even as a young boy, I knew they were being killed. I was three years old, and my father had me watch this cruel process so I would adjust to farm life. Later, when my mother provided dinner for us, I knew what it was and refused to eat. My father forced me to eat a piece of the fresh ham, and afterward, I was fine with it.

I was born in the town of La Plata in Charles County, Maryland. I was raised in a rural area known as Rison, Maryland. By the time I was four years old, I can remember my father in a drunken stupor on the floor, suffering from epileptic seizures due to acute alcoholism. My grandfather, who at the time owned and operated a sawmill, built the house I was living in. This was a small house occupied by a large family. It was on a small farm, with chickens, ducks, pigs, and a smokehouse for smoking hams and other meats, such as bacon. The farm was connected to my great-grandfather's property, a large farm of over 120 acres. My great-grandfather had numerous farm animals, including cows and horses.

When I was four years of age, my parents decided we were no longer welcome on the farm due to our expanding family and my father's actions. His drunken state, along with his unemployment, had finally forced my grandparents to expel us. We traveled around, lived in our car, and finally ended up in Atlantic City, New Jersey. In 1952, I attended the Atlantic City Elementary School. We resided on the inlet, directly in front of the old Absecon lighthouse, which remains there to this day. However, the house we lived in is long gone, now a barren lot. After leaving Atlantic City, we moved to Atlantic Street in Southeast (SE) Washington, DC.

I attended public schools in Washington, DC. The schools were integrated, and it was hard for a child to understand this situation within the public school system and the surrounding public housing. I became a "ghetto kid" in the Highland Dwellings, a public housing project for the poor in Southeast DC, where we resided in an old duplex. Along with my parents, I lived with my four brothers, two of whom were older (Bill and Dennis) and two younger. We fought all the time.

The heating systems where we lived were antiquated coal furnaces with coal bins, which held two tons of coal. At $2 a ton, coal was a luxurious expense for our family, so my brothers and I would take our toy wagon to the local woods and pick up wood to heat our home. Local residents would knock on doors, begging for old soda bottles so they could afford to eat. Money, as usual, was a luxury we did not have. To supplement our income, my older brother Dennis had a paper route in Congress Heights, Southeast, and I had a paper route with the *Evening Star* newspaper in Condon Terrace, Southeast. I also went to the ACME grocery store at Sixth and Chesapeake Street and offered to carry customers' groceries home for tips. On weekends, I would sometimes make up to $8, which was good money for a young kid at the time. My friends and I would scour our neighborhood for discarded soda bottles, which we would take to the ACME grocery for return deposits. To help heat our homes, my friends and I would chase the coal trucks, begging for the workers to drop some coal. Knowing we were all poor, they would drop chunks of coal for us.

On one occasion, the neighborhood kids and I were playing kickball at the back of our residence. One younger boy wanted to play, but he was too young to kick the ball, so I told him no. He ran into his house crying and told his adult sister that I beat him up. She approached me, yelling, "You little White motherfucker!" She began a pinwheel type of attack, digging canals into my face and tearing away my eyelashes in chunks with her fingernails. I was going to fight back, but I had previously been told never to hit a woman, so I continued to block the blows. Finally, she stopped, leaving me a bloody mess and unable to see as my eyes began swelling shut. With my shirt bloody from the attack, I went home to splash water on my face and noticed I couldn't blink my eyes.

As I was washing my face, my mother came downstairs. Seeing my condition, she screamed, "Who did this to you?"

I told her, "The woman across the courtyard attacked me."

My mother ran across the courtyard and entered the girl's house, screaming, "Who did it?"

Police were summoned for a mentally disturbed woman. Once the police saw what had happened to me, they began yelling at the woman who attacked me and asked my mother if she wanted to press charges on her. My mother said she did not, with the reason being that we had to live here and see each other every day. The police warned the woman to never touch me again. I could not see for three days and kept cold wet compresses on my eyes. The canals grooved into my face faded over the years. My eyelashes also filled in, but the memory never fades.

Life at home with an alcoholic father was not pleasant. My father would often become violent, so violent that he would beat our mother in front of us. It was heartbreaking and truly ugly to watch as our mother suffered this punishment, and we were too young and terrified of our father to interfere. When he walked into the room, we all sat at attention, so afraid something would be said to trigger his outbursts with further beatings. When they did start, we would plead for him to stop, crying, "Please, Daddy, please stop." Our cries always fell on deaf ears, and we had to endure the unbelievable brutality of what was being done to us, with no escape. All my mother would do was cry after the beatings, leaving all of us with a broken heart.

I was once outside with my friends and younger brother when an irate Black man began yelling at us for an unknown reason. Being smart-mouthed kids, we yelled back, "Shut up, you nincompoop!" As kids, we went laughing on our way. Neighbors told this man where we lived. He then told our father, who was intoxicated, that we called him a "nigger." My father drove his overdue Diamond taxi to the drug store at Sixth and Chesapeake streets, where he found us and told my younger brother and me to get into the car. I hesitated, knowing he was drunk. I almost ran away but instead got into the car. Big mistake.

He said to us, "When I get you home, I am going to beat the shit out of you."

Upon arriving home, I again had the chance to run away, but being young and afraid, I went inside. He cornered us in the coal bin room, blocking the exit with his body. He removed his belt and struck my brother one time, telling him to go to bed. He then turned to me and said, "You should have known better. You're older."

He began beating me, at first with the belt. He dropped the belt but continued with a frenzy of strikes and blows with his fists. I defecated, urinated, and began vomiting. Then I went into complete panic and tried to squeeze between his legs. He squeezed his legs, holding me as he continued striking me until I was finally able to escape and run upstairs, with him hot on my trail. I got into bed and lay there, petrified that he would continue the beating.

My brother and I were still in bed, battered and bruised, until my mother got home from work. She asked what we were doing in bed. My father told her that he had disciplined us for what we had done.

She screamed, "You put your drunken fucking hands on them!" She attacked him while we tried to stop what was going on. It was the first time we ever witnessed our father being intimidated. She screamed, "You ever touch them again and I will kill you!"

Trying to intervene in this domestic dispute was almost impossible for me as I could barely walk, and it was hard to breathe with what felt like broken ribs, blackened eyes, and a bloody nose. I collapsed, and my mother had to put me back into bed. I couldn't go to the hospital because we did not have insurance.

My oldest brother, Bill, could not take it anymore and moved to my grandmother's house in Indian Head, Maryland. My brother Dennis moved to my aunt's house in Congress Heights. I was left with my two younger brothers to endure our ugly situation. Eventually, my father left home in a drunken stupor, from who knows where. He would return every few weeks, looking like something that crawled out of the woods, begging for a few bucks to continue with his drunkenness. My mother was a waitress at the Hot Shoppes Restaurant in Eastover. She made just enough money to feed us and keep a roof over our heads. She was a good mother to us. At times, she would go to work with blackened eyes. Once, to help ease her burden, I stole a steak from the grocery store so we could have something other than onion sandwiches to eat. I told her I paid for it, as stealing was a no-no. We were hungry. We were all good kids. Eventually, my brothers and I all became civil servants, as police officers, and my youngest brother a firefighter.

At the age of fourteen, I watched my father come home once again to roost on the living room sofa. He stayed intoxicated for a little over two weeks, never getting up to use the bathroom, sitting in his own swill. He had epileptic seizures so severe that he would fall onto glass ashtrays, crushing them and bleeding, throwing blood all over the living room, making it look like a major crime scene. Finally, he asked to be taken to the hospital. At the age of forty-one, he fought the straps restraining him as he struggled with delirium tremens (DTs). Fighting the straps, he broke the bones in his hands and strained his heart, finally succumbing to death. Due to his World War II record, he was interred at Arlington National Cemetery. I was not saddened by his death, but I did not rejoice either. His mother and brothers were present at the funeral, and when the 21-gun salute was sounded, along with Taps, they lost all restraint and began crying uncontrollably for this lost sailor.

My father's nickname was Rudy. He carried this name as far as I know almost all his life. I can remember him chasing my mother with a hatchet in the house at Rison. I saw her run out the back door, shrieking, "Rudy! Rudy!" He threw the hatchet, missing her. I don't know where my grandparents were when this was going on, but I am sure this incident added to the decision that my family had to go.

When we lived in our car, we were constantly hungry. I don't know how we survived, but I do know it was hot. We took off our shirts and stayed in our underwear. My father was, at times, a functioning alcoholic. He held various jobs, with the last one I remember as a taxicab driver in Washington, DC, for Diamond Cab. He had the option to purchase his cab after so many years, and we thought our lives were going to improve with this small influx of money. He once again fell off the wagon when my uncle, another alcoholic, showed up at our house drunk, flaunting a pint of Seagram's 7 and taking shots in front of my father. The next thing I saw was my dad taking a large drink from the bottle, and that was it for him. The story continues with him disappearing for weeks at a time.

During the war, my father was in the US Coast Guard, stationed in Iceland aboard a frigate. His ship was part of escorts for the PQ convoys headed from the US to the Soviet Union. These convoys provided the Soviet Union with military supplies to fight the Nazis. Luftwaffe airplanes and warships out of Nazi-occupied Norway attacked these convoys, creating havoc among the ships. Many sailors were killed by the Nazi's actions. My father was a witness to these things, including U-boats sinking the freighters and leaving men in ice-cold water where they died very quickly. The Coast Guard and Navy ships dropped depth charges to destroy the U-boats, but the men in the water who were still alive had their chests crushed by the explosions, and their lungs were hanging out of their mouths. The sailors protested these actions and wanted to stop the ships to pick up survivors, but it's the old adage "Sacrifice a few to save the many." There were many fights among the men after returning to port and even a murder over the situations they had witnessed. The horrifying events affected all of them. The only thing they could do in port was drink and drink and drink. My father became a constant alcoholic at a young age. Today, these men would be diagnosed with posttraumatic stress disorder (PTSD). The poor guy suffered from his memories of death and could not function in civilian life. My father, along with millions of others, was part of the dark residue left over from World War II.

My family was still living in the house on Atlantic Street. There was something else going on there, something hidden that really scared me—footsteps when no one was there and a shadow of something that used to be there. My mother was at work, and my father had not yet passed away, but he was not at home. My brothers, my friends, and I were playing flip cards against the living room wall. Suddenly, and out of nowhere, we heard footsteps across the upstairs floor and then coming down the steps. We all looked at each other, in fright, with big eyes. We ran for the back door, with all of us trying to get through at the same time. We surrounded the house so whatever it was that was in there couldn't exit without us seeing it. We stayed there until my mother came home and searched the house in its entirety, without finding anything unusual. There were seven of us there, and we all heard it.

Upstairs in the front bedroom, my brother and I had twin beds. One bed was close to the door, and the other bed was next to the window. At night, I could see my brother's bed from the streetlights illuminating the room with gentle light. Night after night, there was nothing unusual. Then, one night, I rolled over and couldn't see my brother's bed. Something or somebody was blocking my line of vision. I slowly looked up to see a man wearing a black trench coat, hands in the pockets, and a big floppy black hat. The most startling and frightening of all were the eyes, glowing black and red with pinpoint pupils gazing at me. There were no other visible features on his face. I urinated and kept saying, "Don't touch me. Don't touch me." I lay there for hours until the sun came up and then ran from the room like a pigeon from hell. This was the most frightening experience I had ever had in my thirteen years.

The twin bed incident is something I have remembered with crystal clarity all my life. Some would say it's my imagination or childhood dreams, but I tell you now that it was completely authentic. I really think and wonder since my father was in the house and was dying if this entity was death, looking for him to touch with its long spindly hands.

As children, my brothers and I made a pact that if our mother died, one of us would kill ourselves to go protect her from our father. We would not leave her alone with him. This is childhood thinking, but it shows the violent lifestyle we were living, and we would do anything to help her even after death.

Later, as I began my personal life, after growing up in a household of domestic violence and questionable history, I realized there was more to being alive. There is something hidden which exposes itself in what is called paranormal activity and raises curiosity about what is occurring "in their realm." Although not all the activity is violent, it can be very scary when you know you are being watched by unseen eyes. The problem with it is…just what is watching you?

In 1965, I joined the United States Naval Reserves and was placed on immediate active duty for two years. After basic training at Great Lakes, Illinois, I was assigned to the USS *Canberra* (Cag-2) stationed in San Diego, California. The ship was assigned to two Western Pacific (WestPac) tours in Southeast Asia. It was while we were in Vietnam that one of our crewmen, while working in the engine room, suddenly came out shouting at the top of his lungs, "I'm not going back in there! You can't make me! I won't do it!"

After he settled down, we asked him what the problem was. He explained there were dead sailors walking around down there with limbs strewn about. Did he ever go back down there? I don't know. But he was very adamant that he wouldn't. We then learned our ship, during the Solomon Islands campaign of World War II, had been torpedoed in that engine room, killing and wounding twenty-two members of the crew.

Our journey across the Pacific Ocean took two weeks, and we berthed in Subic Bay, Philippines. We were excited to finally get off the ship for much-deserved liberty. Olongapo City was exciting to see with its very colorful jitneys. It also had a smell one would never forget. There was a green polluted river-type creek surrounding the town, with young men diving into the swill for money thrown from the bridge. It was disgusting to see these guys diving into this toilet water for centavos or change. A US $20 bill was exchanged for 82 pesos. One peso contained four quarters, or centavos, and a San Miguel beer was 25 centavos. Very cheap.

When we walked through the city in our snow-white uniforms, the Benny Boys, or gay men dressed as women, would start beckoning to us for their services, of course in private. The bars were full of women calling out, "Sixty-nine, sixty-nine," hoping to receive a willing subject. Four of us went to what I thought was a quiet bar and settled down to drink San Miguel beers. At seventeen years of age, I was learning fast and was about to learn more. One of the sailors I was with had been here before and knew exactly what to do. The song "These Boots Are Made for Walking" was playing. This was a cue to bring out the women, not just one or two but twenty-four. They lined up in front of us, prostitutes all. Some were very pretty.

My friends looked at me and said, "Choose one."

I was only seventeen, and all the women were looking at me. I was totally embarrassed and said, "I can't do that."

They said, "You choose, or we will choose for you."

I walked over to the women, found who I thought was the prettiest, and pointed to her. She took me by the hand and led me to a private room where she undressed, first herself and then me. She helped me remove my uniform. Standing there naked, she placed a condom on me and began oral sex. It was my first time being with a woman, and I found her exciting. When I returned to the bar, all the other sailors were laughing. I sat down and laughed too. "More San Miguels, please."

We could only stay in town until almost midnight as we had Cinderella liberty. The ship stayed in Subic Bay for a total of three days before returning to the line, a term used to describe our patrol duties off the coast of Vietnam and our position in combat assignments. It would be another three months before we returned for Cinderella liberty. Sometimes we would go to Hong Kong or Yokohama, Japan, for liberty, but our favorite was Olongapo. While in these ports, each man was responsible to use a cover (condom). If you didn't use a cover, you could contract a venereal disease. I know of one guy choosing to go without, and he ended up with what we called "a case of blue balls." This dumbass finally had to go to sickbay to receive treatment. He did this only after being in excruciating pain in his genital area, and he's lucky he lived.

Life on the ship was monotonous until, suddenly, Klaxons and bugles began sounding general quarters. Shore batteries caught us by surprise. One destroyer took a direct hit in the radio shack, killing men instantly. We suffered one with a head wound from shrapnel.

One evening, while manning our five-inch gun mount on condition three, which means manned but not at general quarters, seven of us were standing outside the mount, listening and watching our main eight-inch batteries shell surface-to-air missile (SAM) sites inland. The cork and smell of cordite were intense. Suddenly, we saw flashes all along the coast of North Vietnam. We didn't realize these were shore batteries shelling us until the last moment. The shells began bursting among us. It knocked off our hats, and we lost our shoes as we began running for our gun mount. Men were screaming and cursing as airbursts were striking the ship, sounding like glass breaking. As I placed the headsets on, I heard the constant beeping to open fire. This beeping continued until all guns were brought into action, with deafening results of explosions and the sounds of returning fire. The ship was still sitting in the sea while shelling SAM sites. It began shaking violently like a major earthquake as it attempted to gain speed to get out of there. Ricochets were everywhere and continued until the ship placed enough distance between us and the shore batteries.

Later that night, under cover of a fog bank, we returned to the position to shell the shore batteries sites using radar controlled five-inch guns. We could hear a low tone of electronic whirring, which would swing back and forth until these eerie noises would suddenly stop, locking onto a metal target and firing a salvo. We could hear the outgoing shells traveling toward the unsuspecting target and then saw the fiery bursts in the fog, with an orange glow and secondary explosions of white phosphorous (a.k.a. Willie Pete or the initials of WP). The shelling continued for hours, wiping out the shore batteries.

After arriving at the Subic Bay Naval Base, we sadly and silently watched the process of unloading dead sailors from a destroyer. It was a somber occasion as silence permeated the area. Some were sobbing for their lost friends. The crying could be heard throughout the base.

When we returned to Vietnam, combat operations continued as the ship fought in blue as well as brown water. The brown water was tainted with the chemical exfoliant Agent Orange. We used this water for showers. It smelled of sewage as it passed cities along its route to the sea. The water even had an oily sheen to it. We would go to sea and bring aboard seawater for desalinization for drinking and cooking.

One early morning, general quarters was sounded along with bugles arousing all of us out of a deep sleep. While responding to my gun mount, I realized just how close we were to the shore observing large rocks within a hundred yards. Above the shoreline, as our ship was sitting completely still in the water, a US Firebase was under siege. In the silence, I could hear the sizzle of flares with their weird light as they slowly floated back to earth. These flares on small parachutes cast light over the entire base and ship, but the eeriest sound was emanating from bamboo being rubbed together by the Viet Cong surrounding the base, creating a noise sounding like "Waaaa waaaa waaaa waa." This sound continued all night long for the psychological effect, announcing their presence without us visually seeing them. We sat at the ready all night long, waiting for an assault from the jungle. The sounds of the flares and the bamboo serenade were unnerving, but we were ready like a cocked gun for confrontation. When the sun rose, they retreated back into the jungle, and we secured from general quarters. This was the strangest encounter we had with the Viet Cong, but we knew the soldiers at the Firebase were ready waiting and absolutely silent.

Once again, general quarters sounded. Only this time, I was in the bath facilities and was about thirty seconds late reporting to my gun mount. I had to traverse under the five-inch guns to reach my assignment. As I went beneath these cannons, they fired, slapping me to the teakwood deck. I was in shock with every bone in my body screaming, and I felt as if my eardrums were rupturing. I could not function for a moment. Then I scrambled to move when the guns fired again, almost knocking me senseless. I continued to try to get from under the guns and finally made it to the hatch. Once inside the mount, I knew they were talking to me, but it was like a silent movie. People were speaking, but all I could hear was a loud buzzing. I had the feeling I had been hit. I finally began understanding what they were saying: "Pass the ammo!"

This life on ship continued until the big day arrived when I was transferred off the ship. I said goodbye to the USS *Canberra* (Cag-2) and was taken by helicopter to a cargo ship to return to the Clark Air Base in Manila. I was waiting with many other military personnel for room on a flight to return home. I was so excited! After two years, I was going home. At sunset, I became chilly and began shaking. A fresh Navy lieutenant saw me shaking and asked me what was wrong. I told him that I was cold. He told me and then ordered me to report to sickbay for malaria. He took my seat home. That bastard! I refused to go to sickbay but still had to wait another twenty-four hours to get on a flight, thanks to the lieutenant. I finally boarded the Braniff international flight full of soldiers, marines, and one sailor, me. The American stewardesses were so nasty to us. They had worked a double shift, poor things. We were all coming back from a war zone, only to be treated like shit. We told them to get away from us, and then the guitars came out, and we all started singing. We didn't see the girls for the rest of the ten-hour flight, and we were very happy to be rid of them. When we arrived in San Francisco, cheers went up. Three hours of sleep a day was over. The black rings around my eyes from lack of sleep took over six months to disappear.

After Vietnam and my time in the service, I met a young lady in San Diego. We were married in July 1967. She had our daughter, who was physically fine. Our second child, a son, was born with a serious birth defect. This defect was expected to end his life by the time he was in his forties. At the age of thirty-two, he contracted a throat infection, which caused his throat to swell shut, suffocating him. My third child, another son, had no birth defects of which I was aware. He passed away on October 19, 2022, at fifty-one years old, from a very aggressive malignant brain tumor. I believe Agent Orange played a role in both of my sons' deaths.

The Veterans' Administration (VA) did not compensate me for Agent Orange exposure until late in my life. Compensation came only after numerous medical studies proved the exfoliant Agent Orange was causing my medical problems.

In 1968, while my wife and I were residing on Front Street in San Diego, California, I broke my right leg in three places. I was at work selling jewelry on Broadway to unwilling service members. When I was on a break, I ran down the sidewalk looking for a coffee shop that wasn't crowded. I did not see the small standalone caution sign located in the middle of the sidewalk. I tripped over the sign. I was flipped in the air and landed on a curb, shattering my leg below the knee with a compound fracture. After being transferred to the University Hospital, the doctor, a Dr. W, attempted to set my leg without first administering any pain medication. I yelled and screamed as they placed my leg into a cast. It was way too tight, and

I began begging for someone's help to loosen it. Nobody came to my aid for hours as I lay there pleading with the nurses, "Please, please help me."

Finally, a young doctor split my cast with a handheld saw, cutting my skin all the way down from my hip, which only added to my misery. The next day, Dr. W came into my room. I had lost all composure and was beyond pleading. I was hurling obscenities at him but was still not given any pain medication beyond Darvon. The doctor told me my leg was crooked and needed to be reset. The doctor warned me it was going to hurt. He was going to cut my cast and place a piece of wood into it, which would force my leg over to the right. When he cut the cast and moved my leg, I screamed and passed out. Still, no pain medication. When I awoke, I was back in my room, suffering in pain and still no pain medication other than Darvon, which is less effective than Tylenol. It was given to me for the numerous breaks in my leg. There was no operation to place metal in my leg. As far as I know, the technology did not exist yet, or I was considered unworthy to receive it. Either way, I suffered for over a year on Darvon. I was living on welfare and needed the cheese line to receive food such as canned chicken (which tasted like fish) and Velveeta. This era in my life seemed to me as just a continuation of all-out suffering that was part of my human existence.

I give no thanks to Dr. W as he allowed me to suffer. I would not let a wild animal suffer like that. After this horrifying experience with my broken leg, I was healed enough to work again. I was employed by the Wilkins Coffee Company as a forklift operator to support my family. Today, my leg is still crooked and scarred, all due to the treatment from this so-called Dr. W.

During my time in the service, I received a military General Equivalency Diploma (GED), as I had not graduated from high school with a diploma. The VA allotted time under the GI Bill to attend college courses on a part-time basis. Therefore, I was able to receive compensation for attending college on a three-quarter time basis, which I did. What I overlooked was that my General Equivalency Diploma (GED) from the military was not accepted by the State of Maryland's Department of Education. A high school diploma is required to apply to become an officer with the M-NCPPC, so even though I had already attended college, my military GED was not recognized by the State of Maryland Department of Education. I needed to take more courses and complete the math section of the Maryland GED test to receive a Maryland diploma. The courses were completed, and I provided the state with a test date to complete the math section of the test. As I knew nothing about the new math which was now being taught in schools and was the basis for the GED math test, I was extremely distraught about where and how to educate myself in a short time.

One of my coworkers knew this type of math and would travel throughout the warehouse where we worked, writing math problems for me to solve onto boxes. I provided the answers and finally achieved a 100 percent solve rate. When my test date arrived, I aced the test and received my diploma. I could not thank my coworker enough. The diploma and acceptance as an applicant by the Maryland Park Police finally provided me with a much brighter future. I had something to look forward to in life and was so excited by my prospects.

I attended Prince George's County Police Academy located in Forestville, Maryland, from June 15, 1973, until I graduated on October 24, 1973. I was teased by my fellow students when I wore shorts during my training. During my tenure as a park policeman, I patrolled all mansions, plantations, and properties owned by the M-NCPPC and joint properties with the Maryland Department of Natural Resources, as well as local governments and Prince George's County.

It is here that my encounters with the unknown and the unseen begin, as well as when my encounters with the nonliving occurred. These were strange phenomena not listed as police reports but as personal experiences. I had an encounter with what I thought was a real person, finding out later it was an entity. It was so real, so disturbing, and so unbelievable. When I discovered the truth, it frightened me, but I had to ask myself, "What was this guy thinking?" That was why he ran. I was in uniform, and his time period clothing told me he thought I was a British soldier trying to capture him or an American soldier with the same intention since he was a British subject at the time.

I now suffer with severe anxiety disorder, for which I have been hospitalized. I have to take antianxiety drugs to calm me down. It is frustrating to know what causes my anxiety yet still be unable to get it under control, even though I know it can kill me. The care of a psychiatrist would probably benefit me. However, it is not one incident but rather numerous incidents which distress me. I need to write these incidents down, or they will be lost forever.

My personal history continues as I attended the Prince George's County Police Academy. My training was interrupted when my oldest brother, a DC police officer, was feloniously assaulted while on the job. Thus begin my stories of criminal activity and unbelievable encounters with paranormal entities. I have entitled the next event "The Survival," and it will begin with my brother's situation.

CHAPTER 2

The Survival

I begin, now, as I remember a situation involving my older brother Bill, who at the time was a detective with the Metropolitan Police Department, Washington, DC (MPDC). This story happened as my career as a policeman was just beginning and adds to the overall situations encountered during my career where I experienced reverse racism. Bill, along with Detective Sergeant Donald Wikert, his immediate supervisor, faced a violent situation that became a life-and-death struggle for no other reason other than they were both Caucasians in a Black neighborhood. Yes, this story is about racism, but remember, it was 1973.

In July 1973, I was in training with Prince George's County Police Academy when I was summoned to the lieutenant's office, which is never a good thing. The lieutenant asked me if I had brothers on the MPDC. I told him that two of my brothers were MPDC officers, both older. He then asked me if I had a brother by the name of William E. Larman. I said, "Yes, my oldest brother, Bill."

The lieutenant said, "I have bad news for you. Your brother is in intensive care at the Washington Hospital Center, and you are excused to go to him."

When I arrived at the hospital, I was met by MPDC officials and fellow officers, some of whom were crying. I was escorted to the intensive care unit where my brother was lying in bed with hoses and lines protruding from him. He had so many tubes in his nose and mouth that he couldn't talk, only look at me and cry. He couldn't even turn his head. Both of his eye sockets were broken, and he was swollen from the waist up from being beaten with a cinderblock. Bill was covered with blood and had innumerable stitches on his head and body. He remained in intensive care for four days. I cannot begin to speak of the heartbreak I endured seeing my brother suffering to this extreme and wondering what the reason was for such a severe beating. Officers on the scene reported Bill and his sergeant, Donald Wikert, were on duty when the incident occurred.

On July 29, 1973, Bill and Sergeant Wikert were working as detectives investigating wiretaps and intercepts when an address of interest came to their attention. It was a court authorized intercept, and the phone books confirmed it was a good address.

The two detectives did not know that this neighborhood within Washington, DC, called Ivy City, was a problem area for the DC police. On that day, Bill was driving my aunt's personal car, a new red Nissan 240Z, while my aunt was driving Bill's vehicle. Bill was planning on driving my aunt's car to her residence, but he and the sergeant decided to drive by the address in Ivy City before dropping off her car at her home.

When they arrived at the Ivy City location, hundreds of local citizens were milling around. Someone in the large crowd saw these two White boys in the red 240Z and threw a bottle, striking the vehicle and causing damage to it. Bill and Sergeant Wikert got out of the vehicle to identify the culprit so a report could be filed with the auto insurance company. As they exited the vehicle, the large crowd immediately attacked them, with one person yelling in Donald's ear, "You ain't takin' the brother!"

Then the beatings began. Bill and Donald identified themselves as DC police officers and displayed their identification, but to no avail. The crowd didn't care if they were police. They only saw White boys in plain clothes. Bill and Don both began fighting back, withdrawing their handguns. Bill was struck in the face by a cinderblock and collapsed next to the car, inviting even more vicious attacks on him. He continued to be assaulted with the cinderblock, but the attackers added sticks, rocks, bottles, and even their feet as weapons, escalating the violence. Bill tried to crawl under the vehicle to get relief from the unrelenting beating with the cinderblock but was quickly losing consciousness. As he tried to regain his footing, Bill noticed blood all over the vehicle, thinking, *My god, who is losing all this blood?"* At the time, he didn't realize he was slipping and sliding in his own blood.

An unknown assailant began prying Bill's gun from his hand. The slipperiness of the blood caused Bill to lose his grip on the handgun, and the assailant took aim at Bill's head to execute him. Donald saw the dire situation Bill was in and knew he was about to be murdered. Donald fired at the suspect, missing him, but the assailant saw Donald and shot, and missed. Donald then relied on his training, so he knelt and fired another shot, striking the suspect in the chest, causing him to collapse. The crowd was able to grab the gun and run away with it.

Donald then ran over to Bill, and they both proceeded to enter an apartment building, all the while being chased and beaten by the crowd. As the officers entered the building, the crowd surged after them, still throwing things, striking the front of the structure and destroying the façade.

As Bill and Donald arrived on the second floor, all the residents were in the hallway. By this time, most of the clothing had been torn from their bodies, and they were bleeding profusely. They began pleading for help and a telephone. After being refused assistance, they took matters into their own hands and forced their way into an apartment while the female resident yelled for them to get out. She said she was concerned for the safety of her kids, but she did have a phone.

Bill and Donald began barricading the apartment door with anything and everything. Absolute survival mode had set in. The crowd in the hallway, screaming racial epithets, was growing as more and more of the neighborhood trickled in to get a chance to kill the officers. The windows of the apartment began imploding, with the floors covered with glass and debris.

Bill called the MPDC communications supervisor, and when a female answered the phone, Bill said, "I need to talk to a supervisor."

She said, "Hold, please."

Bill, almost losing his mind, hung up and called back. The same female answered, and Bill said, "I am a police officer, and we need help immediately." Bill provided the address to her, but she was so upset he had to calm her down to get the information across to her.

MPDC units from the Ivy City vicinity responded and saw a large crowd attacking an apartment building, but they didn't see anyone who looked like a police officer and canceled the call. In the meantime, Bill and Donald believed they were going to die as everything was imploding on them. Bill made another call to communications with further information as to who they were looking for, and the officer in trouble call was reissued. This time, Donald tore away the barricade and ran down the steps into the crowd, who assaulted him again. He screamed to the police, "We are over here!"

A corridor of police officers was formed leading into the building. Bill, still in the apartment, believed Donald was being attacked, so he tried to leave the building but collapsed in the hallway. He had almost given up when the door opened and, thinking he was about to be attacked again, prepared for the worst. Bill saw a pair of uniform pants coming in, and he knew his ordeal was almost over. The arriving officer, upon seeing Bill, exclaimed, "Look what they have done to him!"

Other officers assisted in placing Bill into the back of a police cruiser and began transporting him to the hospital. At first, they were headed to Providence Hospital. It became clear that Bill's injuries required the expertise of the Washington Hospital Center, where he was admitted into the intensive care unit.

Sergeant Wikert's ordeal was not quite over yet. As he was entering the back seat of a police cruiser, someone in the crowd saw his service weapon protruding out of the back of his pants in the small of his back, grabbed it, and ran into the crowd. His weapon was never recovered. By the time Bill Larman's handgun was found, it had been utilized in four different homicides in Washington, DC. The weapon was what other officers would call tainted, as in cursed to serve.

Donald's physical injuries consisted of cuts, bruises, and loss of all his dental crowns. He was treated at the hospital and released. However, there was something else Donald would suffer from, which was PTSD. A person cannot endure such an attack without something physically and mentally going wrong.

Bill suffered severe head injuries, including a concussion, crushed sinuses, broken eye sockets, and numerous stitches from his waist up. He was swollen beyond recognition and had to be on life support for a couple of days as a precaution. Doctors at the time predicted correctly that he would suffer severe sinus problems later in life. This prediction came true, and he also suffers from severe headaches as a result of the beating he received.

The 240Z they had been driving was destroyed by the crowd. The tires were flattened, windows knocked out, with dents all over the exterior from being struck by stones, bottles, and other missiles. The tags were stolen, the interior destroyed, and there was blood all over it. The apartment building was another story. The façade needed restoration, and the interior was damaged beyond belief by a misguided crowd.

Still, today, close to fifty years later, Sergeant Donald Wikert and Detective William E. Larman have trouble speaking of this incident. They faced a life-and-death situation, branding them with a sore that will not heal. Understandably, a verbal conversation about that day's events is very upsetting to them. I feel for them as I, too, have faced dark situations that never go away. You think about it for the rest of your life. It enters your dreams just like the soldier in combat you never forget.

A local newspaper published an article after speaking with one of the outstanding citizens within Ivy City, which stated, "Two white, plainclothes police officers entered the neighborhood, stopped, stood on top of the 240Z and started shooting children. We had to stop this, so we attacked them."

According to the phone company, the address in Ivy City provided by the wiretap and intercept was not the correct address. The correct address was in Northwest DC, and the phone books were wrong.

When Sergeant Wikert was in the fight for his life, there were so many people trying to hit him at one time that nobody could connect with the ultimate punch, which allowed him to remain on his feet. At the same time, Bill was continuously struck by the cinderblock, causing him to collapse. If both had collapsed, they would have ended up dead. This incident is a living, haunting memory for them.

Now we begin with my stories of ghostly phenomena and other tales. The first is an actual encounter with whispering entities and phantoms explaining the deadly details of what they were going to do to President Abraham Lincoln.

CHAPTER 3

The Occultations

Mary Surratt House and Museum
9118 Brandywine Road
Clinton, Maryland 20735
301-868-1121

During encounters with the occultations at the Mary Surratt House and Museum, I never observed any that appeared to be scenes from a horror movie. Instead, the apparitions were performing their conspiracies until their end. They were not waiting to pounce on or frighten you, as the observer. They were continuing with their daily plans and activities. There was one occultation that was different from the rest, and it was a poltergeist. It did not want me, as a police officer, or anyone else, causing problems in the house and interfering with whatever its afterlife assignment was, making the house a very scary place. Maybe the poltergeist did not realize it had passed on, or maybe it just wanted to continue with what it was doing. It had frightened employees out of the house, and some had resigned their positions.

First, we need a little history of the United States, the house, and how the conspiracies that took place within it might have happened.

At the end of Civil War, it was estimated that as much as half of the currency in circulation was counterfeit. The Secret Service was established in 1865 as a branch of the Department of the Treasury to take counterfeit currency out of circulation and help protect the US economy. After President William McKinley was assassinated in 1901, the job of protecting prominent political figures was added to the Secret Service's responsibilities.

During the 1850s and early 1860s, it was a generally accepted practice for people to leave their doors unlocked, and the White House was no exception. Anyone could walk in and approach the president, his family, and any dignitaries that might be present. During this time, protection for the president consisted of a secretary and one policeman.

In 1865, Washington, DC, was a major encampment of the Union Army and was the seat for the Army of the Potomac. There were many high-ranking military officers in Washington, and they were flattering President Lincoln for favors as the war seemed to turn in the Union's favor.

The story behind the Mary Surrat House began during the Civil War. It became a Confederate conspirators' nest, at first to kidnap the then president of the United States, Abraham Lincoln. The kidnapping did not happen as Mr. Lincoln failed to go to where the conspirators were waiting for him. Two weeks after the attempted kidnapping, Union forces took over Richmond. It was largely believed when General Robert E. Lee surrendered at Appomattox Court House, the war was over, but that was not the case. There were other Confederate armies in the field, and the war continued. Lee's surrender was merely the beginning of the end. The kidnappers, thinking the war was over, now planned to assassinate the president. There were still over ninety thousand Confederate troops in the field.

The house in Clinton, Maryland, was an inn, as well as a home owned by John and Mary Surratt. It was the center of all the plots against the president, and it was here all the whisperings began and have not ended, continuing as if the Civil War was still being fought. John Surratt was also the owner of a home located at 541 H Street, Northwest, Washington, DC. Mary decided to make this home a boarding house and was residing there at the time of President Lincoln's assassination. However, she visited the inn in Clinton on the afternoon before the assassination, which was planned for April 14, 1865, at Ford's Theater in Washington, DC. Mary brought a rifle and field glasses to be hidden there for John Wilkes Booth, who would call that very night.

The conspirators at the Surratt House came to light when John Wilkes Booth, in his flight after killing the president, stopped at the inn in Clinton. He then journeyed on to Dr. Mudd's house for treatment of a broken leg then on to his demise in Virginia. During the time before the assassination, there was a tremendous amount of whispering in this house. Sound traveled a long way during the early part of the war, with no planes, trucks, cars, or telephones. Horses and wagons on rutted roads made for very loud noises, and snow increased the sound effects. The house did not have insulation, so whispering was a must. A person talking normally an acre away could be understood.

After Mary and her coconspirators were captured, they were convicted by a military tribunal and then sentenced to execution by hanging. Mary became the first woman ever to be convicted of murder and hung for her dirty deeds. Her last words on the gallows were "Don't let me fall." The reason for this statement was simple. These gallows were over twenty-five feet high, and being afraid of heights, she cried out.

Over the years, the Surratt House became dilapidated and on the verge of collapsing, when it was renovated and restored in the early 1970s by the M-NCPPC. Before it was restored, I remember seeing this house collapsing on itself with the rear wall being the only one still standing. During its renovation, a Sharp's Carbine rifle was found attached to a wire hanging down within the wall. The rifle became a museum piece. After the restoration, a small reception center was constructed for visitors. The house itself had a small office upstairs, which was staffed.

During the 1990s, I received a memo for me to check on an employee working in the house by herself. I stopped by early one afternoon, and as I attempted to enter, I found the door was locked. Since the house was now a museum, and it was during business hours, the door should have been unlocked. I knocked on the door. The woman answered, and I introduced myself and asked why the door was locked. She became upset, telling me people were entering the house, walking up and down the steps, wearing old 1800s-type dress, and they were not visitors. She also reported noises, footsteps, and people whispering.

I asked her, "Are you alone here?"

She said, "Yes."

At that moment, we heard a huge crash upstairs. I asked again, "I thought you were alone here?"

She said, "This is what I am talking about. It goes on all day long."

I ran upstairs and found exactly where she'd been sitting at her computer. A 2' × 4' ceiling light fixture had fallen on top of her chair. If it had struck her, it would have caused critical injuries. This employee lasted two more weeks and resigned.

The Surratt House is, in my opinion, and I am not a paranormal investigator, one of the most active haunted houses and includes a poltergeist within. After conversing with other officers, they tend to believe something is there, including visions of people, whisperings, curtains moving with candlelight at night as if something or someone is looking out at you, and other occurrences. We as police do not write reports on ghostly activity. We only speak among ourselves. My personal experience begins with the following incident, which is a true story.

I was working a midnight shift in the southern area of Prince George's County, which included the Mary Surratt House in Clinton.

About 4:00 a.m., I received a dispatched call for a silent alarm activated by motion within the Surratt House. Upon arriving with my headlights out, I parked in the rear parking lot, looking at the outside of the structure for any visible signs of breaking and entering. I parked far enough away not to alert anyone inside the building that I was there. I informed my dispatcher I was on the scene and would check the outside perimeter for obvious broken windows or doors.

After checking the exterior and seeing everything was normal, I asked the dispatcher if they were still receiving the alarm. The response was "10-4, it is activating in the interior foyer area." I then decided to enter the house since I had the master key to the rear door. I unlocked the door and entered, locking the deadbolt behind me so no one could follow. I proceeded to search with my flashlight in one hand and my handgun in the other, warning constantly for anyone there to come out. I could see the motion detector in the foyer still ticking.

After searching the entire house, I found nothing unusual. I informed my dispatcher to continue to hold me inside checking a little further. During my search, I saw some old letters from the 1800s, and since I am somewhat of a history buff, I holstered my handgun and began reading them. While reading one of the letters, something touched my right ear, and I thought it said something. I turned around and saw a moth flying around the still ticking motion detector, thinking to myself this was probably what activated the alarm. I began reading again, still holding my flashlight, which was impairing my vision as to what was around me. The brightness of the paper in the low light almost blinded me. Once again, something touched my ear and whispered something. This time, I dropped the letter, pulled my handgun, and swung around, expecting to see someone. Nothing was there, so I holstered my weapon.

It was at this moment the whispering began in earnest in both of my ears. The touch of unseen lips upon my ears was not only frightening but also chilled me to the bone. It was aggravating, and I could not stop it. I tried to cover my ears, yelling, "Stop it!" to no avail. In my haste to exit to the rear door, I had locked myself in. I dropped my key ring and had to leave my ears exposed, allowing the whispering to continue until I could find the correct key. I had to try each one in the lock until I located the right one. When I stepped outside and locked the door, the whispering suddenly stopped. What a relief! I sat in my police cruiser for a few minutes and stared at the house while I gathered my senses as to what just occurred. I cleared the call by informing my dispatcher, "It was just Mary moving around. Unknown causes for alarm."

This incident is just one of my personal experiences. Each time after this, I expected anything to happen while in the building. There are other officers with their own stories of fright. This house has numerous phantoms residing within.

The current historian of the Mary Surratt House informed me the building is very haunted. She personally stayed overnight in it on two different occasions. She stated that as long as these phantoms did not touch her, she was fine listening to the sounds and whispering. I then reminded her of the employee who resigned due to poltergeist activity that was occurring.

The same historian informed me there have been séances held in the house, including a government-sponsored one. The séances were conducted within the last several years with the results finding, "Mary is not in the house." She is located at Fort McNair, where she was executed. The activity at the house is very sad and very energetic. I again told the historian the employee that resigned was working inside the house every day. She was subject to noises and physical abuse by these phantoms. The historian is working in the office, not in the house.

As I interviewed the historian a little further, I discovered she was in the house with other people who were talking, laughing, and basically having a good time. The activity in the house exposes itself when the house is silent. The people staying in the house are not silent. They're walking around, giggling, wanting something to appear.

I am not convinced there are no phantoms residing within. I have had my own experiences, as have other officers within our agency, continually observing and hearing these things 24-7, 365. One or two nights spent here is insufficient to discover these occultations.

One summer afternoon, I was having lunch at a local fast-food carryout near the Surratt House. Another dispatched call came in requesting assistance for trespassers at the house. I responded and was there in less than two minutes. The employees in the office informed me there were unauthorized persons walking into the Surratt House when there should be nobody there. I walked over to the house and went in. I searched the entire house and found nothing. When I informed the employees that nobody was there, they were astonished. They walked over and entered the house themselves, finding no one. I cleared the call as unknown.

These are not unusual calls for this property. People see things which are not real, but they believe they are.

The Surratt House has one very conspicuous thing in common with most old houses and mansions. The one thing is silence. The dark residue, which resides within its walls, was once alive. These people were representatives of a government that failed. That government was the Confederate States of America. These people believed in that government and committed their conspiracies within the house. Succeeding in executing the president of the United States of America, they thought they were doing the right thing for their government. After all, they were still at war and probably still are.

During the 1980s, students were allowed by the M-NCPPC to reside in the house on the first floor. It was during daylight hours that there was a police dispatched call to southern area park police on patrol to respond to the Surratt House. Upon arriving, the student living there told the two officers that an intruder was walking around upstairs. The officers stood still and listened and heard someone walking around upstairs. It's true. Someone was there. Officer Frank proceeded to go upstairs, searching from room to room, looking for the intruder. He cleared all the rooms except the last room on the left. He proceeded to the entrance and peered in. He didn't see anyone, but there was a large indentation on the bed, as if someone was lying on it. The hairs on the back of his neck stood up. He called for Officer Sam to respond to the room. When he told Officer Sam what he saw, they both looked back at the bed. The indentation was gone…completely vanished, and the bed was perfectly made.

Further searches were futile. There was nothing there. The call was cleared as unknown noises.

The reception building, where the historians greet you as you enter and explain the house's history, contains numerous artifacts. Evidently, this building has become haunted, too, due to the antiques located inside. This building, although not attached to the Mary Surratt House, is located on the property next to the house, and it is conceivable that this, or other entities, may have entered it. All current park police personnel entering the Surratt House are aware of the powerful hauntings that continue to manifest. It is a very scary place with many historical connections.

I do think time and dates on the calendar are of considerable importance as to when these entities or shadows begin to expose themselves. During certain months, the conspirators met with associates staying in the house. After all, it was an inn.

It is unknown whether a property which once contained buildings, warehouses, or other structures since destroyed by fire, demolition, or other means is still haunted or possessed by entities or shadows within. When the structures are gone, is the dark residue still in the area, or has it been released from its afterlife of possible torture?

The Surratt House may be a prime example of entities remaining on a property even when the original structures are gone. The house was collapsing on itself when it was restored by the M-NCPPC. Once it was completed, the entities returned, or maybe they had never left. This old house was in very bad condition, so where were these entities or phantoms then? Do they occupy a space where something once was, even if it was on the second or third floors or more? For example, in Gettysburg, Pennsylvania, there are floating entities where houses destroyed during battle once stood. There were soldiers who were killed inside. These ghostly shadows remain, it seems, where they were killed, even though the original structure is gone. This is not to say victims who were killed or murdered stay where they were slain. If it were me, I would want to go home, as I am sure most of us would want to too. But I'm not sure we have a choice.

The occupation of structures that no longer exist may include the Twin Towers in New York City. These people were only going to work, not war. These phantoms will be over our heads, if they are not already, going about their unseen business. Whatever it is, I used to be a nonbeliever. Do not try to convince me otherwise now, especially as you read on.

As employees can attest, the Surratt House continues to have entities appearing, even in daylight. They are seen as regularly as clockwork, people traversing to and fro, their mode of transportation unseen.

I continue my career with these encounters in the next story, which I titled "The Entity." This is a ghostly phenomenon and an actual encounter with an entity of absolute clarity and stunning reality when observing what it did.

CHAPTER 4

The Entity

Darnall's Chance
Formerly the Buck House
14800 Governor Oden Bowie Drive
Upper Marlboro, Maryland 20772
301-952-8010
Friday through Sunday, 12:00 p.m. to 3:30 p.m.

This old mansion was built circa 1742. When I first encountered it in 1976, it needed, and was scheduled for, restoration. We, as the Maryland Park Police, routinely patrolled it even though it was just an old building. The mansion has an extensive history, including suspicious deaths which occurred inside.

The first floor of the house was previously boarded up by the M-NCPPC. On our routine patrols, we always checked to make sure the plywood boards were in place and no one was trespassing on this property. No trespassing signs were posted all around the house.

In 1781, Maryland became the seventh state of the United States to ratify the Articles of Confederation and Perpetual Union. Darnall's Chance was built in 1742, thirty-eight years prior.

The name Darnall's Chance was created by Colonel Henry Darnall (1645–1711). According to English law, the colonel was required to provide names to certain parcels of land for tax purposes. Darnall's Chance was one of those parcels. Over time, the colonel acquired large tracts of land, eventually accumulating twenty-seven thousand acres in what is now Prince George's County, with holdings in four other counties as well.

Mr. James Wardrop, a Scottish merchant, purchased six and three-quarters (6 3/4) acres from Colonel Darnall's son, Henry Darnall II, in 1741. Mr. Wardrop built a fifteen-room brick dwelling, which was originally one and one half (1 1/2) stories high. In the nineteenth century, Mr. Wardrop married Ms. Lettice Lee.

The house then passed on to Mr. Edward Crafton W. Hall. Mr. Hall owned and resided there from the late 1800s through the twentieth century. Then, in the late twentieth century, Mr. Harry Buck Sr. purchased the mansion, which he sold to the M-NCPPC in 1974 because of its historical value.

In 1987, a burial vault was found in the rear of the mansion. The vault contained the remains of nine people, buried under eight feet of trash, which had accumulated from the eighteenth and nineteenth centuries. Throwing trash into the vault showed complete disrespect for those interred there. Buried in this vault were the remains of Ms. Lettice Lee and two additional adults, along with six children, five of whom were Native Americans. At the time, the disrespectful treatment of the vault was unknown, but it would be revealed later.

After purchasing this property, Mr. Harry Buck Sr. discovered a sinkhole in the backyard, not knowing it was the burial vault. Because of the yard's dangerous condition, he would not let his children play there. There was another danger in the backyard. It was believed ghostly activity was occurring there, including transparent apparitions which frightened Mr. Buck and his children.

The house itself was also found to have abnormal activity in it, even during daylight hours. In the 1950s, Harry Buck Sr.'s son, Irwin Buck, adopted a little girl. As the years progressed, while playing in the house, she began hearing and seeing entities. She became frightened, especially at night. The activity included sounds such as talking, screaming, walking, and other unidentified noises. She was also warned not to play in the backyard due to a pit "that would swallow her." When she played in the storage cellar as a child, she had no idea what was mere inches away under the fallen bricks. Then, in 1987, the pit was discovered.

On routine patrol one day around 1:00 p.m., I found the front plywood door of the house had been forced away from its frame. Believing there were trespassers inside the building, I requested a county police K-9 unit to respond to the location. In the early 1990s, K-9 units could still be utilized to help forcibly remove unknown persons from buildings. When the Prince George's County Police K-9 Unit arrived, the handler attempted to have the dog enter the building, but it refused to obey the command. At that point, the K-9 officer physically picked up his partner and tried to enter the building, but the dog became highly agitated, bit his handler, and attempted to run away.

Another K-9 was requested and dispatched. This canine reacted differently to the situation by immediately responding to the handler's commands. The dog was heard snarling and snapping on the second floor, as if someone was in his grasp. As the handler and I responded to the second floor, we fully expected to see someone the dog had found. Instead, the canine was attacking an unseen entity that was by the fireplace, biting into thin air. The other officer and I looked at each other in amazement, wondering what the dog was doing. The canine did not listen to commands while being pulled off his unseen prey. The handler finally dragged his canine partner away, allowing us to examine the entire fireplace and chimney area with negative results.

On another routine patrol, Officer JJ and I found the plywood on the front door torn away again. When we entered the foyer, we could hear someone walking in the upstairs hallway. It sounded like gravel and debris were crunching under his feet. I silently whispered to JJ, "He is right there." I was pointing to the top of the staircase.

Believing this time we were going to apprehend the suspect, JJ went to the parlor stairs, located to the right of the foyer, while I began to silently ascended the main staircase. As we were climbing the stairs, the walking sounds continued.

When I arrived at the top of the main staircase, I saw an unknown male facing away from me. I immediately shouted to him, "Police! Hold it right there! You are under arrest for trespassing."

As I gave the command, he turned toward me, totally surprised. He was a White male in his midthirties, with wide-open brown eyes, clean-shaven, with three-inch-long black hair combed straight back. He was wearing off-white seamless button-up pants with two top buttons unfastened and a light gray tassel shirt that was open at the neck.

This person immediately turned away from me and ran in the opposite direction, running toward JJ. As JJ began to enter the room, this person ran completely through him. I could not believe what I saw. JJ did not see this happen to him at the crucial moment because he was looking in the other direction.

JJ asked me, "Where is he?"

I said, "He ran through you."

JJ said, "I heard running, but that's it."

We believed we were finally going to make an apprehension but found no one there. All we found was a ghostly entity that had escaped from us. This episode scared and confused us at the same time.

Several years later, the Buck House was scheduled for historical renovation. Located in the cellar of the house was an oval-shaped brick storage area utilized for perishables, including vegetables, wine, and fruit products. The bricks of the cellar began dropping onto the floor and, over the years, accumulated into a large pile. During the renovation, these bricks were removed, and a human skeleton from the nineteenth century was discovered under them. Today, you can see where the floor has been bleached to remove the stains.

When the skeleton was discovered beneath the bricks, Prince George's County Police Homicide Unit was notified. Work was halted until the police investigation was finished, delaying the completion date of the renovation. Because the case remains an open homicide investigation, no information about it is available to the public. However, it is known that the bones of the skeleton were becoming fossilized, indicating it is an old site from the eighteenth or nineteenth century. There were neither fleshy remains nor the normal stench of rotting meat.

I did speak with the historian at Darnall's Chance, and she does not believe in ghosts, even after listening intently to details of my confrontation before the renovation. She stated she has never seen one there. She also denied a skeleton was discovered beneath the bricks, but she was not present when this occurred.

During renovations at Darnall's Chance, everything was rearranged from what we, as officers, remember. We were not responding as tourists but in police mode. Now upon entering the house, there are mannequins in little rooms on the left, where previously it was just a large empty room. The staircase has been removed and relocated to the rear wall, and the entire second floor was removed. Even the fireplace is gone. All this rearranging makes it difficult for anyone to see or picture where our interactions with this entity took place.

Officer RG reported for day work one day in the early 1980s. A new officer, Officer JJ, asked RG if he could ride along with him since his regular field training officer (FTO) had called in sick. These two officers were on routine patrol and decided to do a property check at Darnall's Chance, then called the Buck House. The mansion was boarded up with plywood all the way around, having a lock and chain through the front plywood door. RG wanted to show JJ the interior and explain to him why it was under lock and key. It was to keep hobos out. RG had the master key and unlocked the chain. Both stepped inside to see the layout of the mansion. RG immediately heard someone upstairs walking in the hallway at the top of the steps. He told JJ to go to the other stairwell and proceed upstairs while he would go directly up the main staircase. This would allow the unknown person to be apprehended for trespassing. As RG placed his foot on the stairs, he heard heavy boots running down the hallway toward JJ. JJ heard this person running toward him and came out of the rear stairwell to capture this person. There was nothing there.

A county police K-9 unit was once again requested for trespassers within the mansion. This time, when the dog was released, he ran into the living room next to the foyer and began howling. The howling continued for no less than fifteen minutes. The dog had to be coerced into leaving the mansion. Another extensive search was conducted with nothing found except old copperhead snakeskins.

It must be noted this entity did not display any hostility toward us, even when I confronted him. I believe it is a very docile phantom going about its business, whatever that business is. I actually feel sorry for whoever it is that might be trapped within the mansion, walking there forever. This entity roamed here long before we approached it. He was used to solitude, and I feel for his loneliness.

Mr. Hancock Lee, Lettice Lee's brother, was related to the Lee family of Northern Virginia fame. He is one possible suspect of being the entity within the mansion. He might be upset about the disrespect shown to his family in the vault, with all the trash thrown into it. Mr. Lee almost perfectly matches the description of the man I saw. At his death at thirty years of age, Mr. Lee was five feet and six inches, with a slim build, black hair, and dark brown eyes.

When the renovations of Darnell's Chance were taking place, the entire second floor was removed. That included the fireplace where the then unseen entity was encountered by the Prince Georges County Police K-9 Unit. All the action and disturbance, including my own and other officers' interactions, made this solo and very dejected soul who wandered the mansion, possibly for centuries, a celebrity of sorts among police officers. He never knew exactly what was taking place, only that his lonely existence was interrupted by officers and today's visitors and historians, wishing to travel back in time to experience his prior life, as he knew it. Now that his once final resting place under a pile of bricks in the oval basement has been removed, he has no knowledge of where his remains now lie.

All this continuing activity in and around Darnall's Chance has made him a very cautious entity, no longer showing himself as in the past. What used to be dead silence is no longer silence at all. He has fast become the reluctant ghost, but…he is still there.

CHAPTER 5

Governor's Bridge

There are many stories of ghostly phenomena with Governor's Bridge. I can say with utmost confidence that it is more than haunted.

In the 1700s, the bridge at Governor Bridge Road was a wooden causeway that provided the British provincial governor, Samuel Ogle, access to Anne Arundel County from Prince George's County over the Patuxent River. The bridge expedited the many trips by Mr. Ogle to and from Annapolis. Governor's Bridge was also utilized by farmers to bring their products to market. The river was navigable by wooden ships as far north as Queen Anne Town, which was located a little farther south than where Route 4 exists today.

During the war of 1812, the British Navy launched the Invasion of 1814, which ended in the burning of the United States presidential residence and other US federal office buildings. Right after the Battle of Bladensburg in Maryland, the invasion culminated with the Battle of North Point and Fort McHenry in Baltimore. The Patuxent River is where it all began, including the writing of "The Star-Spangled Banner."

To date, there have been a total of three bridges constructed at this location on the river. The first bridge was damaged beyond repair around 1817. The second bridge was constructed after Anne Arundel County commissioned Mr. Joseph Stockett and Mr. James Saunders to build another bridge of better quality, which remained standing for over a hundred years. In 1912, a third bridge was constructed, which is still standing today.

Governor Bridge Road shares what is now a large intersection with US Rte. 301. During World War II, US 301 was a two-lane road that was made of concrete. The sand and gravel used for construction were mined from a location on Governor Bridge Road near the bridge. Route 301 north and south was a military highway utilized in the war effort. The highway was dedicated as a "Blue Star Memorial Highway" to honor the Armed Forces of the United States. The bridge was not used by the military due to weight restrictions, but it did provide shortcuts for employees during the highway's construction.

Years passed, and the war is now a memory, along with the gravel area by the bridge. All that is left are the old drive-up scales and construction debris. The area once again became isolated, a place where fishermen trudge on worn-out paths along the river, searching for the perfect fishing spot. The area around the bridge is a very swampy lowland. When it rained, it was closed due to flooding along the road. Now the area is closed on a permanent basis, blocked by large concrete barricades that make access almost impossible except by foot.

There are stories of ghostly activity in the area and, supposedly, a baby crying nearby. Also, a country song was written entitled "The Ghosts of Governor Bridge Road." The property and the surrounding area are owned jointly by the M-NCPPC and the Maryland Department of Natural Resources and are closed to the public. For years, I traveled back and forth across the bridge while on patrol. At night, I would turn off the car engine and, with my windows down, just listen to the sounds around it. I heard farm animals from the Anne Arundel side but also things I couldn't explain. I never heard a baby crying, but I did see little lights flashing around like lightning bugs, but only in February. There were, and still are, sounds I cannot explain, such as echoes of something sounding like kittens crying and gurgling noises.

Over the years, I have seen results of gruesome murders near the bridge. The one murder that stands out in my memory was that of an African American woman who had been dismembered, her torso becoming entangled on a fisherman's line. The fisherman thought he had snagged a log until he realized the log was wearing panties. Not all this unfortunate victim's extremities were found—just one leg, one arm, and a cardboard box. The box had hair in it, but her head was not recovered. It is believed that animals dragged it off, but it could be at the bottom of the river.

The perpetrator of the crime left behind a policeman's treasure trove of evidence. He should have just left his name and address under the bridge. On the Prince George's County side, a large clear plastic bag was found. It contained newspapers he used when he dismembered her, a hacksaw, and Miller beer bottles with his chewing gum inside. He was chewing gum while he cut her into manageable pieces.

The murder was solved after all the evidence pointed to him. He was a congressional aide, and the woman was his mistress. He provided her with a condominium located in Southwest Washington, DC. It was in this condo that she attempted to blackmail him by threatening to expose him to his colleagues and family. This threat sealed her fate. The aide attacked her, stabbing her five times in the back and killing her. He then began the gruesome work of dismemberment with the hacksaw, later found at Governors Bridge. After slicing her up, he placed her parts into a large trash can, and with a hand truck, he took the can with its contents right through the lobby of the condominium. He took the time to speak with the security guard on duty, telling him the can contained very heavy old books, and he was on his way to get rid of them. At one point, he even offered the guard one of the books. The man succeeded in placing the can in his car and then drove to Governor's Bridge. Some of the woman's extremities were found farther east on the Choptank River, southeast of Governor's Bridge, on the eastern shore of Maryland.

When all the puzzle pieces came together as to who committed the murder, homicide detectives went to the condo in DC, searching for him. When the detectives left the building, they saw the suspect outside sitting in his car. As they approached, the man knew it was over. He placed a twelve-gauge shotgun under his chin and effectively blew off his head. The murder-suicide completes this episode, except for notifications of saddened families and the dark residue left at Governors Bridge Road.

In the summer of 1987, a young lady was kidnapped from Allen Pond Park in Bowie, Maryland. Her vehicle was found in the parking lot, and an immediate search of the area was conducted. There was no trace of her to be found and no witnesses to her disappearance.

Investigators received information that the young woman was taken to Governor Bridge Road. A search of the area by members of the Maryland National Capital Park Police Mounted Unit smelled the stench of death near the bridge. Days had passed since the young lady's disappearance, and time was of the essence. The odor became stronger, with insects gathering in the area.

Finally, on the left-hand side of the bridge, before crossing into Anne Arundel County, a grave was discovered. Homicide detectives were summoned, and the exhumation of a body from this insultingly shallow grave was conducted. The body was identified as the female kidnapped from Allen Pond. She was raped and murdered right by the bridge and then buried there. I cannot obtain any information on open homicide cases other than the investigation is being conducted by Prince George's County Police.

I can positively say this area is haunted. The murders committed here are continuing today. The residue of crimes of previous murderers is there. I patrolled this area for years during the 1980s and 1990s and know these things are occurring here. It is now a very isolated area and was even more so in the eighteenth through twentieth centuries. What went on here is never going to be discovered. It was wide open for anyone wanting to dispose of his or her dirty deeds. Years ago, this area was so quiet that anything could occur here. More and more people had access to the bridge, and they used the route to throw items from it, leaving behind their murderous debris.

From my experiences, where wetlands or swampy areas exist, there can be thousands of frogs croaking at one time. When they suddenly go quiet, you know something else is around you. Even the crickets in summertime go silent as a warning that something is there. The most unnerving experience, though, is when the birds suddenly go quiet, and I mean dead silent. Usually, this happens during the day, but I have been through this experience at other times. You can hear a pin drop in the woods. Owls being in the area may be the cause of this eerie silence, or it may be something else. These types of occurrences seem to happen more frequently near the bridge. My only advice is to stay alert. There is one other type of danger around this bridge, and that is humans with guns. People go there to shoot their weapons. Due to the isolation, they feel unrestrained.

I did watch a video providing a narrow view of a supposedly ghostly figure wearing a topcoat and a floppy hat. It is a silly video of a girl screaming constantly because of the figure, at first on the bridge and then following her home and into her house. To me, having weapons within my residence, I would have ended this figure where he stood.

CHAPTER 6

Old Hyattsville Courthouse

(Precinct)

Old Hyattsville Courthouse
4990 Rhode Island Avenue
Hyattsville, Maryland 20781

This old building has an extensive history, although it is no longer used as a courthouse. It now houses states attorney offices and other offices within the court system. The basement was the Prince George's County Police Precinct for the Hyattsville Division of the Department, and the sheriff's department had a cell area located downstairs next to the old commissioner's office. The downstairs area is no longer utilized, and it was darkened on my last visit.

In the past, thousands of arrests and fights took place there, along with the murders of two Prince George's County police officers. The police officers' murders remain a sensitive subject to this day. The fellow officers, friends, and relatives who are still alive very clearly remember what happened here. I will not mention the suspect, or should I say the convicted killer's name, as he does not deserve recognition. I will say that years later, he died by his own hand.

I have friends telling me not to go into the basement as there are noises, voices, and other things going on down there. You can even hear these activities from other areas in the building. The property belongs to the State of Maryland, and trespassing infractions are strictly enforced. The only way to enter is by requesting permission through the State of Maryland, but don't count on approval to enter. The building continues to be a place of business for the state.

When I was a District Court of Maryland bailiff assigned to the newer courthouse, we as bailiffs could enter the basement of the old courthouse. There were very spooky noises emanating from there, even during daylight hours. We did not enter the area at night as it was under lock and key.

It was in the Hyattsville Precinct in the basement that, on June 26, 1978, two Prince George's County police officers, Albert Marshall Claggett IV and James Brian Swart, were booking a theft suspect. These two officers, at that time in 1978, did not have lockboxes to safely store their weapons. They wore gun belts with their weapons in the holsters while booking all prisoners. The suspect grabbed Officer Claggett's gun, shooting and killing him. Officer Swart then came into the room to assist Officer Claggett, and the suspect killed him as well. The fifteen-year-old suspect was just a street punk and was sentenced to only twenty-five years in jail. He was paroled after serving only seventeen years. In my mind, this injustice was carried out due to him being a Black child while the officers were White. The Black community stated that the White officers were beating a Black child, although that was not true. He was a criminal and proved it for the rest of his wretched life, committing suicide after he and his brother carried out an armed robbery at a bank.

I praise officers Claggett and Swart for their performance of duty with the Prince George's County Police. I attended the funeral services for these two fine young officers, and it was a somber occasion when they were laid to rest at the Gate of Heaven Cemetery in Montgomery County, Maryland. Still today, I feel for the families of these two young men whose lives were cut short.

The murders of these officers in the basement of the old courthouse have added to the injustices that were carried out here. There is no doubt this place is haunted, and it was haunted before these murders. The officers' murders have just added to it. It is a sorrowful situation that two quality officers are gone, with their souls left here to haunt the basement due to the injustice started by a worthless individual. The court system adds to the misery by allowing a group of misguided protesters to influence the supposedly responsible court system. These were decent police officers who were protecting us from this type of killer. Fifteen years old or not, he should have faced the death penalty, which was still in use at the time. Instead, he was exalted by the Black community as some type of worthless hero protecting himself from the aggression of two White police officers. This assertion was a total farce. This community was protecting a criminal, that is all. I certainly hope the two officers have been saved from this dreadful situation.

As a policeman, I would bring prisoners to the District Court of Maryland Commissioner's office. The entrance to the precinct was located on the second floor, with a set of steps leading down into the precinct area. Many prisoners fighting with police officers fell over the railing, landing with a sickening thump. Some received broken bones while others sustained concussions. Several ended up in critical condition. I don't know how many suffered death, but it was likely some did die.

These incidents add to the noise emanating from the area. I became involved in fights with prisoners who were under the influence of drugs or alcohol. Some would try to commit suicide and refuse to be presented to the commissioner, causing more problems. Thumps are heard inside this area, along with human noises such as moans and groans. It is not pleasant to hear. These sounds will continue until the building itself is finally torn down. But even then, will the sounds remain?

CHAPTER 7

The Salted Lot

Original location:
3807 40th St.
Cottage City, Maryland

Current location:
3210 Bunker Hill Rd.
Mt. Rainier, Maryland

At first, I believed the history of this lot began in 1949. But I found the background began long before then, as it became entangled with the War of 1812 and the Battle of Bladensburg in 1814. This small vacant piece of property is now owned by the M-NCPPC. As a Maryland National Capital Park policeman, I wanted to know the property's history since I had to patrol it. The historians within the M-NCPPC provided as much information as they could. Many stories have been shared about this lot over the years. This telling is my version of events and begins in the early 1800s. Nothing has been written connecting the property to the occurrences I am about to relate until now. As the story unfolds, the soldiers of 1814 come alive again at the Battle of Bladensburg.

On August 24, 1814, the British forces were aligned against American troops in Bladensburg, Maryland, five miles northeast of Washington, DC. The British forces first landed at Benedict, Maryland, on August 19, with a little over four thousand assorted troops consisting of four Infantry Regiments, a Royal Marine Battalion, naval detachments, and freed slaves recruited as Colonial Marines. The British also had a new type of weapon, the Congreve rocket. Although it was a very ineffective and unreliable weapon, it struck fear in opposing soldiers when it was deployed at close range. British troops also had another weapon proven in battle—the long triangle-shaped blade of the bayonet, which would leave a gaping hole in a soldier's body almost impossible to close by doctors at the time.

As the British forces approached Bladensburg, an impressive seven thousand United States forces were waiting. The Americans were composed of a hastily formed militia, a mostly civilian force, and a couple of hundred regular army forces. The militia usually provided "one-shots" before retreating. Before most of these one-shots were ever dispensed, the British began firing their rockets, which had never been seen before by the Continental Army troops. Terror and havoc spread through the troops, and they were forced to retreat.

After the battle, the British suffered 64 dead and over 180 wounded. The US forces lost over 12 men, with 40 wounded and over 120 captured.

As the American Army retreated, they left their soldiers where they lay. In their zeal to win, the British did not attend to their soldiers either. They quickly advanced, leaving the men behind to suffer and endure the reality of what was going to happen to them. The dead and wounded on both sides were left to suffer their fate, alone.

The walking wounded could and would follow the army while the American militia went home. The battlefield was littered with screaming and crying men suffering from large nasty battle wounds or broken bones. All of them were in agony. They began dying from thirst. When a human suffers a major injury, the body goes into shock and demands water. Because their wounds were so horrific, they were unable to crawl toward the Anacostia River to quench their torturous thirst. They began dying. The summer heat, high humidity, and blood-soaked ground began attracting various insects. The flies and yellow jackets were eating their flesh, adding to their misery. Then larger predators arrived. Dogs and birds of all types began eating the soft parts of their bodies, such as their eyes. The men couldn't protect their faces due to the wounds to their extremities. They slowly died, crying for mom and God to save them from this terrible fate.

When the British Army finished burning government buildings in Washington, DC, and began returning to their waiting ships in Benedict, Maryland, Mother Nature had a little surprise for them. As if in punishment for what they had done, a black storm front approached with howling winds, sideways rain, and trees crashing down. It was almost as if God was telling them something.

The storm, with its howling winds and soaking rain, did not miss the moaning wounded men. It gave them a chance to quench their thirst. The relief was brief, though, and the suffering returned the next day. Now the men were soaking wet. The high humidity and torturous temperatures made their misery worse than it was before. They must have been wishing themselves to die to end it.

Many years passed, and urban sprawl began filling in on both sides of what is now known as Route 202, Landover Road. Total disrespect has been given to these dead soldiers. Their bones, uniforms, and weapons are completely ignored or not seen by passersby. This land should have been hallowed ground, but instead, it has been left open to such insult.

One day, at 3807 Fortieth Street, Cottage City, Maryland (the original site of the battle), a new home was constructed. The construction workers were pouring the basement concrete and allowing it to dry when they thought they heard something under the concrete. They ignored the sounds, playing them off to outside noises.

Once the residents inhabited the house, something began occurring in the basement. There were strange sounds emanating from under the concrete. At first, it was muffled sounds, which became cries, then moans, gradually becoming continuous screams.

Furniture began moving on its own, with see-through apparitions arising through the concrete floor. The house became occupied by a poltergeist.

The residence had a thirteen-year-old boy living within. He became possessed by an evil entity, which forced the family to move from this house to one located at 3210 Bunker Hill Road, Mount Rainier, Maryland (current location). The only problem with this move was it was not far enough away from Cottage City. Mount Rainier is a little town right next door. In 1949, the events that were occurring became the actual story of *The Exorcist*. It was not a girl but a boy. The movie premiered in 1975, and as in all movies, it was more fiction than fact.

The poltergeist at 3807 Fortieth Street followed the family to 3210 Bunker Hill Road. Its manifestations became even more disturbing with never-before-seen entities and items being thrown. The teenager was so possessed, he had to be restrained and forcibly taken to Georgetown Hospital in Washington, DC, for examination by their doctors. After numerous examinations, he was cleared of any physical abnormalities. Then the psychiatric evaluations began with the same result: no mental abnormalities.

The Catholic Church became involved as it was deemed the boy was suffering from demonic possession. A priest from the Saint James Parish of Mount Rainier was assigned to the teenager to confront the evil spirit(s) within him. There were over thirty performances of the exorcism ritual conducted, with the child being transported to St. Louis, Missouri, for special exorcisms. It was during one of these rites that the teenager ripped open the bedspring mattress, retrieved a bedspring coil, and slashed the priest down his arm. This feat had to have taken incredible strength, especially since the boy was restrained. Possession by an evil spirit does not necessarily give someone superhuman ability, especially if he only weighs 132 pounds. I have questions about what was going on in that room for these events to have happened as told. A person cannot, no matter how strong, rip open this type of mattress.

The Speculation

There may be another side to this story, which cannot be proven now but can be thought about considering the recent events that have occurred within the Catholic Church. There have been convictions of predatory priests performing unwanted sexual acts on altar boys, which may have some bearing on this story. We do not know the background of the priest other than he is, or was, a priest. He spent a lot of time with this fourteen-year-old boy, even staying with him for long periods in hotel rooms, supposedly providing support for his condition. The church is now known to have a very real reputation for hiding problems with priests, although this fact was not widely known in 1949. At that time, it would have been considered blasphemous to think of priests in this manner. It seemed they were having a free-for-all with their victims, and the church was hiding it. It is possible the boy was a victim of abuse, and this situation was not made public at the time. However, these are just the thoughts of someone looking at these events as an outsider, an older policeman who attended sex crimes school. During my career as an officer, I dealt with the reality of sexual crimes and with sexual predators covering their tracks.

After these incidents, the house at 3210 Bunker Hill Road (current location) was blessed from room to room with holy water. In the early 1960s, the house burned down. When the debris was cleared, the Catholic Church blessed and salted the ground. The salting of the lot was to prevent evil entities from returning. A gazebo was erected on the lot, but children and adults refused to use it. Eventually, the gazebo was removed, and a playground was erected. Children do not play on this lot as their parents have warned them of what happened there.

What is not discussed is the forgotten or overlooked situation at the Cottage City (original) location. Although the lot at 3210 Bunker Hill Road was salted, what about the other lots or businesses within the battle zone? They, too, have something occurring, although it is muffled by human activity. This little town is where it all started at the beginning of United States history, and its ground has not been blessed or salted. The population is residing among these spectral figures.

To read further, the "Debunking the Myth" of 3210 Bunker Hill Road, Mount Rainier, Maryland, titled "The Haunted Boy" of Cottage City, Maryland, is available at Strange Bookshop, parts 1 through 5. The above is their version of events, but it did not include the "Battle of Bladensburg."

CHAPTER 8

Blue Pond

Blue Pond
Muirkirk Road
Laurel, Maryland

There are many unused gravel pits throughout the state of Maryland. They are usually leftovers from strip mining projects abandoned by the profiteers. The Blue Pond in Laurel, Maryland, is the exception. Mother Nature forced it to be abandoned when it was flooded by an unknown hidden source of water. One story was that the bottom of the pit fell out into a hidden cavern. Either way, it filled with water to an unknown depth. There is speculation that this pond of crystal clear water is haunted. I do not doubt this idea.

The Blue Pond is owned by the M-NCPPC. It is closed to the public and is so posted. This area was once a mining pit that supplied the marble for all the federal buildings in Washington, DC. This area is secure and has been so for years. It used to have a locked gate at the entrance on Muirkirk Road, which citizens would just drive around.

As park police, we would drive back to the pond and break up the parties being conducted along its banks. Getting back to the pond at that time was fairly easy. On seeing it, the pond was not very big, but it was very deep. Some stories exist that the bottom fell out of the pond after the excavation of an underground cavern. The depth of the water is unknown. At times, the water is crystal clear. You can see where the water is shallow near the banks and then drops off, with tiered levels at the south end. You can still see where an old access road led into the pond. On the west side is a high hill of fill dirt that was removed from the pond. I used to drive my cruiser to the top of it. The east side is a level wooded area where people would swing out and dive into the pond. The north side is very marshy with lily pads full of frogs and largemouth bass.

At the south end of the pond is a remaining access ramp to the mine. One day, when the laborers reported for work, they saw the floor of the mine was filling with water. Evidently, they had struck a spring. The machinery in use at the time is still there, having been abandoned due to the rapid rise of the water in the pond. The workers made many attempts to get the mining equipment out of the area but were unable to do so, and the machinery was left on the access road. I know a diver who dove into the pond. He said he saw the equipment on the ramp at a depth of about sixty-five feet. I also know fire department divers wanted to use the area for training purposes but were later deterred because of what is called tea, meaning the water was too cloudy for training purposes.

In the late 1970s, a person was reported missing in Blue Pond. All rescue efforts were exhausted with no recovery of the body. I was told that kids would swing out over this pond and drop themselves into the water. They didn't know it was a spring-fed pond. In the summer, the water on the top is warm while less than four feet down, it is ice-cold. A shocking reality.

It is best to leave this area alone. I agree with the M-NCPPC's decision to close it and leave it that way. I am writing about it because it does exist and is extremely dangerous. There are no signs to identify exactly where the pond is, only the "hundred block" of Muirkirk Rd.

One hot summer night in the late 1980s, an officer working a midnight shift found, at approximately one in the morning, a station wagon parked at the entrance to the pond. After notifying the dispatcher of his location, the officer noticed there was fishing equipment in the car. He naturally thought someone was at the pond. At this moment, he was startled to feel cold wet hands on the back of his shoulders and turned to confront a nude wide-eyed male yelling something. The officer's reaction was to strike out, and he hit the man in the face with his flashlight. The flashlight broke, and the batteries scattered along the road. The nude person began screaming, "Don't die, Dave!" and was jumping around on the road. Then he suddenly ran down the path toward the pond. There was no moonlight this night, so the road was very dark. The M-NCPPC had also cut down numerous trees which were blocking the path to the pond.

The officer called for assistance, and when a young Prince George's County policeman arrived, the park policeman was still picking up the batteries to his flashlight. The park police officer informed the county officer that he thought there was a drowning back at the pond. The young county policeman began running down the path, hurdling the fallen trees by the light of this flashlight. Being young, he could hurdle the trees. The older policeman, not so much. He had to climb them.

When the park policeman arrived at the pond, he found the county policeman's clothes, gun belt, vest, boots, and hat on the ground. The young officer was swimming out to a rubber raft, where he could see two people. The county policeman's sergeant and lieutenant then arrived on the scene and asked, "Who is that in the water and on the raft?"

The park policeman informed them that the two on the raft were unknown, but the guy in the water was one of theirs.

The lieutenant began yelling to his officer, "Get the hell back over here. What the hell do you think you're doing? The pond is dangerous. Get out of there!"

It was discovered that three men were out fishing all day and were finishing their trip by smoking marijuana, swimming around the raft, and diving into the water. One of the men, named Dave, dove into the water and never surfaced. It was at that time the Maryland Park policeman came upon their station wagon.

Rescue operations began immediately but were slowed by the numerous felled trees that had to be cut and removed. It then became a recovery operation, which began at daylight when the divers entered the abyss. One diver descended to a depth of 110 feet with no bottom in sight. The depth was registered on his equipment. As he ascended, he discovered the body in 12 feet of water, with hands clasped in front of his chest, appearing as if he was already in his casket. This finding ended the recovery process.

The wet naked male who approached the officer from behind was not one of the two men on the raft. Dave was the victim in this incident. It is unknown who the man, yelling, "Don't die, Dave!" was. Speculation was that the wet naked man was the drowning victim, and he ran through the trees to go back to himself. Oddly enough, when the victim was examined, he was noted to have contusions on his face, as if he had been struck with something. The other two men on the raft never left the pond to make any notifications. They never saw anyone else at the pond until the young county officer appeared.

The Blue Pond may be haunted. After all, people have died here. It used to be deep in the woods, very secluded, and was not watched or monitored. At night, there is nothing to provide light, and even in the daylight, it is very scary. As police officers, we were called to the site for a disaster of some type. We were not there to experience paranormal activity. This particular incident reminds me of a watery "Sleepy Hollow."

CHAPTER 9

The Incident

This story is a short account of an incident that occurred during a routine patrol. I was searching for criminal activity in a gravel pit but found something totally unexpected. It frightened me, so much so that I activated my emergency equipment.

There are many gravel pits in Prince George's County. But the one that stands out in my mind is the Suitland Bog. Four roadways, as well as apartment complexes, border the bog. The roadways are Pennsylvania Avenue, Suitland Parkway, Suitland Road, and Silver Hill Road. This area was once a strip mine, leaving mounds of gravel behind. There is an electrical station located on the Suitland roadside with very large high-intensity power lines running through the pit. The pit was used to make the concrete used to build the Suitland Parkway. There is, within the area, a piece of property owned and managed by the M-NCPPC. It is not a park but rather a special property. What makes it special is the variety of carnivorous plants such as Venus flytraps that grow there.

The gravel pit is a magnet where stolen vehicles are stripped of their parts, as well as a site to commit other crimes. It was here, one hot summer night, that I had an encounter I will never forget. Patrolling this property while working midnights was a must for me. I entered the area with my headlights out and used my parking brake to stop the car to avoid alerting anyone else who might be there committing crimes. As I approached the access road under the high-intensity power lines, there was a pale blue light, at a very low altitude, coming from the direction of the electrical station. I came to a complete stop, placed my car in park, and continued to watch the light as it came toward me at an ultra-slow pace. Thinking this was a stolen car entering the pit, my initial reaction was "Got one." But it became clear that what I was seeing was something else, something a little more mysterious.

Whatever it was, I was ready for some action. I perked up to high alert before realizing something different was happening. The light was being cast from above the power lines, making a light blue glow onto the lines. I exited my cruiser to get a better look at it and saw a round cylindrical type of lamp with a large electrical bulb of some sort with vertical links within. The light being emitted was causing the lines to glow while it was directly over them. I expected to hear a helicopter traveling over my head or some other type of noise. There was no such sound, not even a whoosh from the wind. Then suddenly, as the light was positioned directly over my head, illuminating me in the light, there was a very loud click. The light shut off, and there was nothing but lightly glowing lines. I expected to see whatever this thing was. After all, it was only about twenty-five feet above the power lines. But there was nothing there. I became so scared that I activated all my emergency equipment and exited the pit as fast as I could. The gravel pit is only three-quarters of a mile from Joint Base Andrews. There was no military response from the base, so they obviously were not aware of this incident.

I could not discuss this incident with anyone for fear of being ridiculed and made to look like a fool. Holding the rank of corporal, I would have lost all credibility. Weeks later, I confided in an individual who I thought to be trustworthy, only to be betrayed. He informed everybody that I was seeing UFOs, which caused the activation of a clique of skeptics. They requested a meeting with me to explain what I had seen, but their minds were already made up about me and the incident. I could not say anything about it without sneers and snickers. I finally said, "I know what I saw. I just cannot explain it." Then I turned and walked out, letting them believe what they wanted. Nothing I said was going to convince them otherwise. It is funny, as for several weeks after that, there were other officers confiding in me about unexplainable things they had seen too.

I was reluctant to go into the pit at night for a long time after that. I could see into it, watching for glowing power lines, which would be a telltale sign the object (or whatever it was) was there. These lines only glowed when the UFO was directly over them. I never saw it again, but then again, I didn't want to either.

I do not want to sound like I'm exaggerating about these things that have happened to me in the past and that are continuing to do so. I am just relating these events as I experience them. For years, the world's militaries officially would not admit and even ridiculed the existence of UFOs. Now all the militaries appear to acknowledge that UFOs are real. What changed? These objects are intelligently operated and move at amazing speeds and maneuvers that create large inertial forces. The human body could not withstand such forces.

The United States Navy was involved in a recent incident with one of its most advanced fighter jets. This was brought to light during an inquiry of the jet's pilot and a female navigator. While on a mission, the jet, at a classified speed, was approached by a UFO, which began maneuvering around this fighter as if the craft was scanning the jet. The navigator and pilot attempted to place the UFO in a vulnerable position, but the UFO outmaneuvered the fighter jet and kept it that way. This action by the UFO unnerved the navigator. The pilot spoke of this incident, but the navigator did so only in anonymity.

Their testimony, together with film footage, provided a very enlightening experience for the "advanced fighter," making it look antiquated compared to the UFO. The jet did not stand a chance against the unknown craft. We need to advance our technology, or we are lost as a race of beings. The episode I am speaking of was named the "Tic-Tac" incident. This UFO, or UAP (unidentified aerial phenomenon), displayed incredible acts of speed and inertia, including coming to a standstill just above the surface of the ocean. On the surface of the water, it began roiling, and something could be seen under the water's surface, appearing to be another monstrous Tic Tac. Suddenly, as if it knew it was being watched, the UAP disappeared, one above the surface, the other below.

Since these things do exist and are seen daily, it was not surprising that I saw one. But I did not expect to see one this close, and what was it doing?

One night, while working a midnight shift in New Carrollton, Maryland, my supervisor asked, "Did you see that light in the sky jumping around? You could not get a fix on it."

I replied that I did, but I had just ignored it. Years later, I became acquainted with an adult who, as a child, had been raised in Greenbelt, Maryland. He and other local kids would go camping in the Greenbelt Agricultural Center. At night, they would just lie down and stare at the stars. He and his friends noticed the same light jumping around in the sky. I could not believe he was telling me this same story of the UFO that I saw in New Carrollton. I told him I saw the same UFO, but I was in New Carrollton at the time. As the crow flies, that is right next door.

There is another incident involving UFOs that occurred in Russia. Twenty-four civilians opened fire on some UFOs that had landed in a "nest" of unknown flying objects located in a large outcropping of rock. The civilians were armed to the teeth, with one .50 caliber machine gun and numerous other weapons. A video recording of the incident showed hundreds of UFOs fleeing the area while dodging rounds of ammunition fired from the guns. The video also shows multiple tracers striking and ricocheting off the rocks, throwing out sparks like fireworks. Several of the UFOs were destroyed, but one landed near a group of civilians. Five beings emerged from the object and began to glow. The beings shot rays of light at the people who were watching, turning twenty-two of the twenty-four into pillars of stone. The two survivors were horrified as they watched their fun turn into a nightmare of retaliation.

I do not have any further information on what action the Russian authorities may have taken to punish the survivors. Since the Russian government received information and intelligence from the recovery of the UFO remains, maybe they believed the people involved had suffered enough and left them alone.

One day, my wife and I visited our beach house in Selbyville, Delaware, where I called her attention to the jellyfish floating in the canal to the rear of our residence. These jellyfish were clear in color, except for one outstanding feature. They glowed sporadic green light, flashing continuously. I said to my wife if this little jellyfish could fly in the air, it could be a UFO. It was fascinating to actually hold it in my hand and watch this display of green lights flashing within it. There were many of these jellyfish in the canal, and I watched them for a long time, not knowing how they did this. If there exists in the ocean depths these types of jellyfish, but of enormous size and far advanced intelligence than us, and they could withstand pressure and inertia residing within the ocean for billions of years before us. They could have the knowledge that we humans seek with flying abilities millions of years ahead of us. We as humans have existed on the earth for only several hundred thousand years. Compared to them, we are like lowlifes how we consider rats or mice with very low intelligence. However, the human race is probably surprising them with our science in such a short period. The only thing left to express their mental capacity is the power to promote a powerful force to fly through the water or atmosphere just by thinking it. Incredible as it may sound, there is no other propulsion system visible except by thought, enough to create this energy with vessels able to withstand the thought process. The maneuvers these UFOs display, I believe, is created by mental telepathy so powerful that it is incredible. Just think it, and you are there. The crafts utilized by these creatures have to be filled with some type of liquid for them to withstand outstanding maneuvers providing a safe conduit within to protect them. This is just a thought on how they could possibly do it. There is no other explanation, and their weapons could be far more advanced than anything we possess.

These incidents, along with other encounters not reported here, are and have become extremely dangerous. We may need to rethink how to approach these types of interactions with the unknown. Although the Russian incident showed the unidentified crafts may be vulnerable, human civilians were grievously harmed.

What follows next are stories of the incidents that occurred during my career which were, and are, very odd, especially "The Screaming Lot."

The Incident at Lake Baikal

There are many believers as well as skeptics of unidentified flying objects (UFOs). After observing reports on all these objects, I tend to believe the only living creature that could survive the inertia and pressures of ocean depths, as well as zero gravity, are jellyfish. They could be highly intelligent forms in existence within and over our oceans for an undetermined amount of time. The interiors of these crafts could be a type of liquid in one form or another to allow incredible displays of these objects.

In England, crop circles are considered a form of artwork with some displaying incredibly detailed work of jellyfish. How would an alien know what a jellyfish looks like? I believe these UFOs are from this planet. It makes you wonder where they are located. The jellyfish crop circles could be a self-portrait.

Recently at Lake Baikal in Russia's Siberian Mountains, seven divers were separately performing underwater experiments when they suddenly noticed being observed by three beings wearing strange-looking helmets and having frog-like feet watching them. These "things" resembled human beings but were over eight feet tall. When one of the divers attempted to capture one of these "things" with a net, all seven divers were suddenly blown to the surface of the lake at the exact same moment by an unknown force, resulting in the deaths of three of the divers. Their deaths were due to their blood boiling nitrogen, creating a decompression sickness known as the bends. The Russian government began conducting large investigations at this lake, but because Lake Baikal contains more fresh water than the Great Lakes combined and the depth of the lake is over one mile deep, human divers are unable to descend without the use of robots with lights and cameras. This incident and investigation are now considered to be top secret but can be viewed on the television series *What on Earth?* airing on the Science Channel.

The one item these UFOs and USOs have not displayed is if they are armed. There have been incidents where aircraft have disappeared after encountering these objects. If "they" have some type of defense or offense system, they have not been revealed yet. With millions of years to perfect any type of defense, chances are they would be far more advanced than ours. The fact that the divers at Lake Baikal were blown to the water's surface by an unknown force could be a type of defense mechanism.

Humans have created offensive weapons from gunpowder and then nuclear, creating diverse types of destructive forces. This is our only type of basic material to provide these weapons. There is no telling what damage the objects can do. We had no reason to fire upon them and could only imagine what the response and repercussions would be.

The reason for mentioning Lake Baikal is because of my incident in Suitland, Maryland, and all the unexplained occurrences throughout the world.

CHAPTER 10

The Screaming Lot

There were numerous antiaircraft sites across the United States left over from World War II. They are gone now, but this one site had a hidden and very loud side to it. I am about to share with you what was going on here. This site gave us all, citizens and police officers alike, goose bumps. What happened here to cause the sounds is unknown. Citizens and police came to know this area as the Screaming Lot.

When I first became a park policeman, I knew of a World War II antiaircraft site in Oxon Hill, Maryland. At the time, this site was one of the scariest places I had ever encountered, mostly due to the screams that could be heard in the area. At first, we thought the commotion was just teenagers playing their games. After interviews with the teens, that was found not to be the case. They were too scared to go near the place due to the screaming. At the time, it was believed the sounds were from an animal; cats such as bobcats cry out loud, and some fox calls sound like a human female. These beliefs were later found to be untrue. But first, let's delve into how I knew about the site.

In the early 1950s, my family had relatives residing in Potomac Heights, Maryland. Since we lived nearby in Washington, DC, we traveled to visit with them on a regular basis via Route 210, known as Indian Head Highway. At its intersection with Oxon Hill Road, there was a large military installation located on the southwest side of Route 210. My two older brothers and I would ask my father what this site was, with sandbags stacked over four stories high and large guns on top of them. He explained to us that it was an antiaircraft site left over from World War II. It was built there to protect the DC area, including the Torpedo Factory in Virginia, as well as the mansions on Oxon Hill Road.

I began patrol duties in 1973 when I was assigned to the southern area of Prince George's County. We were using the county police radio since my agency was still young and on a low budget. One night, calls began to come in reporting "screams in the woods" emanating from the old antiaircraft site. Since a portion of this property was M-NCPPC property, I was assigned to investigate these calls, along with other county police cars.

The site, or what was left of it, was a series of concrete underground bunkers. The sandbags and large guns had been removed, revealing a semi-barren site covered with brush and small trees. The calls continued to come in for screams coming from the area of the bunkers, or what we thought were the bunkers. This area was checked, but nothing was found or heard, and the call was cleared.

Then on different occasions, citizens began calling for screams in the bunkers again. I would respond to this area and just listen without exiting my vehicle. I, too, began hearing the screams. They were very loud, echoing throughout, sounding as if a large animal was trapped inside. I then called for other units to respond to my location. Once again, after thinking I had solved the problem, nothing was found, but the wails continued.

Somehow, or so we thought, people were finding a way in and out of the bunkers and playing pranks on us by shrieking and playing hide and seek. During an interview conducted by the police with one of the callers, it was discovered that these were not prank calls.

They were coming from a reliable source, emanating from Oxon Hill Manor, an M-NCPPC property with private residences within.

It became so scary, raising hairs on the back of my neck and producing the largest goose bumps I ever experienced. Thinking back, the screams, along with the howls that were also heard, sounded like those of a mythical banshee that was somehow trapped inside and panicking to get out. Whenever we received calls for the screams, we responded, believing somebody might be hurt. The calls were never ignored. The situation reminded me and other officers of "The Boy Who Cried Wolf."

At times, I could hear these noises just by pulling my car over on Route 210, Indian Head Highway, with my windows down. The screeching sounds were incredible. We thought if two or more officers would stand there, whatever it was that was screaming would be quiet. Boy, was that ever a mistake. When the screams began, it put chills in all of us who were standing there listening to it. It was not just a scream but a cross between a howling scream and a prolonged cry that slowly faded. It was very, very frightening. We thought these noises might be coming from underground tunnels. Or they could have been emanating from the lot itself due to something unseen that occurred there years before. At times, the noises were so loud I had to cover my ears while expecting to see something rising out of the ground and showing itself. There were no bird, insect, or animal sounds heard in the area. It was truly scary.

We never lingered there, especially after dark. It was unnerving, with sounds surrounding you in every direction. The source of the sounds could never be pinpointed. They just seemed to come from everywhere. We would stand there with guns in hand as the screams began, sounding like the yowling of the werewolf in the movie *An American Werewolf in London.* It was extremely frightening. Whatever occurred there, while unknown, must have been truly horrible.

Since the 1970s, a parking lot for Metro Transit and an office building were constructed on part of the lot. Later, the rest of the lot became part of the Tanger Outlets, which included shops and large parking lots. The area was filled in and covered by construction debris, likely muffling the sounds.

Oxon Hill was known for its hog farms. Every year, the slaughtering of these animals was a necessity to meet consumer demand. This area could have been a farm, being so close to Route 210, for transport to Washington, DC, markets on Florida Avenue, Northeast. If not immediately silenced, hogs scream very loudly when they're being slaughtered. It is a very brutal process. The screams and howls emanating from the lot could have been a leftover sound from the hogs being killed. The sounds have somehow remained there like a haunting. Maybe the reason the men deployed at the antiaircraft site did not notice the sounds and other activity was because the area was an active farm. Most soldiers in World War I, as well as the World War II eras, were born or raised on farms and were used to farm sounds. Television was not invented until the 1920s, and TVs were not found in homes until the late 1940s and the early 1950s. Radio was a common form of communication before the Korean War.

The Screaming Lot, in its original form, is no longer in existence, though it is still there, buried away. I still would not put a stethoscope on it to listen. You might be horrified by what you may hear. I personally have heard enough from this lot to last and scare me for a lifetime. The calls for service were emanating from Oxon Hill Manor, an M-NCPPC property with private residences within.

CHAPTER 11

The Pastor

"The Pastor" is a story of suffering and heartbreak for a man of God and his faithful wife. Having lost his ministry late in life, he was unable to establish another one due to his age. With no income other than the charity of others, he and his wife faced poverty and profound disappointment. I felt for them. They lived a life of devotion for the Lord and denied themselves a life of luxury, only to suffer in their older years. They never lost hope, even until the bitter end.

I was having a lot of religious turmoil in my life at one time. I was baptized a Lutheran, but my current wife is a Catholic. I did not start attending church until she came into my life. Once we began a relationship, I started attending church with her. I then realized what I was missing in my life—companionship and a belief I had not realized that I had in Jesus. With participation in the church, I had something more to guide me through my career and life. I was still a policeman with a foul mouth, and I am still trying to stop this vulgar habit. No matter what I said or how hard I tried to stop it, the language just flowed out of me as if it were meant to be.

Early one afternoon in September 1991, I was on routine patrol in the southern area of Prince George's County, Maryland. I received a dispatched call to check on the welfare of a homeless couple in a vehicle in the Tanglewood Park on Woodyard Road in Clinton, Maryland. When I arrived, Officer RG met me there. We saw a vehicle parked in the middle of the access road, occupied by two elderly people with a small white dog. The interior of the car was loaded with personal items, as if they were moving.

When I spoke to the driver, I learned he was a pastor from the Midwest who had lost his ministry. As we spoke, I could see his eyes welling up with tears. He and his wife were traveling around, hoping to find a new place to begin another ministry. He began his story of despair and told me of his failure, even to the Lord, to maintain a ministry in his name. This pastor was so heartbroken over his failure. I could feel his pain. Their despair touched me deeply. As he was crying, I could see the frustration of total disappointment in his soul. He was truly beyond asking for forgiveness. Due to his age, he had almost lost all hope of ever having a new flourishing ministry.

I felt my heart sink as he spoke. I could do nothing to help him other than to palm him a little bit of the money I had in my pocket. He gently grabbed my hand and began thanking me, telling me he would pray for me. I almost cried myself. The other officer saw me give the pastor the money and said, "You're just a big softie at heart."

We left the park wishing the pastor good luck. When I was about half a mile down the road, I decided to go back and give the pastor my last little bit of money, knowing I could make it up again. When I returned, they were gone. I searched nearby restaurants knowing they were hungry and then looked in gas stations, with no luck finding them.

Later that evening, I stopped at a convenience store on the way home. Seeing the lottery machine, I bet $5 on the Maryland Match 5 game, thinking nothing of it. When the drawing occurred several days later, I won the $50,000 prize. I could not believe it, and I began thanking the pastor for praying for me.

Approximately ten years later, I was having a dream when suddenly, in the middle of this dream, I heard, "Larry, Larry, what are you doing?" A familiar elderly gentleman approached me, but I could not place how I knew him.

I responded, "Yes, sir, what can I do for you?"

He said, "You're cussing too much."

I was startled at first, but suddenly, it came to me. It was the pastor, and he was warning me about my foul lips. I realized he was an angel now, giving me a warning and some guidance in my life.

I still attend church with my wife, and my cussing is still out of control, which I believe is from years of dealing with the negative side of life. I do remember what the pastor looked like, and I could point him out today. I also know that he and his wife have passed on. I hope they have finally received their heavenly reward since life was so hard on them. God bless you, Pastor. You and your wife were truly people of God.

Although I believe in Christ and his teachings, I have to function here on earth and in this reality. I was hired to provide assistance to and the protection of our citizens. This process includes me being able to kill someone without self-remorse. I will have to face afterlife retributions for doing just that, but it is what is required to protect our society from criminals. Somebody must do it. I know I will have to explain my actions after I am gone. These things I do bring automatic punishment in the afterlife, as they violate the commandment "Thou shalt not kill." I have never been unjust or brutal. Sometimes people force you to be physical with them, and most of them deserve it. I have seen brutality, and I mean brutality. But I never participated in it, and I am left with a clear conscience.

As I explained in previous chapters, bad situations exist where violent confrontations have occurred. They could be within mansions, houses, barns, or even open fields. We as humans must understand there is an ultimate power to whom we must answer when we are gone. There will be predetermined assignments in the afterlife based on our actions in this life. We cannot escape the consequences, except for our religious beliefs. Those who do not believe in the ultimate power will suffer the fate of eternal damnation. Those that do believe will not suffer that fate, but they must pray and ask for relief to free their souls of sins to receive this forgiveness. I truly believe this principle; otherwise, I would not have seen or experienced the things I did. I was presented with special views, like the old movie *A Christmas Carol*, only mine were actual encounters, not fictional stories. The nonbelievers will return as ghosts or phantoms of those who previously existed, drawing the living as spectators to their demise.

My next story is of very brutal situations I witnessed and in which I was involved.

CHAPTER 12

The Brutality of It All

The following stories under the "Brutality" section are hard subjects to read, but they are the truth and a difficult way to understand what is really occurring behind the scenes. There are many more I could write about, but I have selected some of the worst to include here. These are some of the most brutal memories I have experienced. It is reality.

Miscellaneous Mayhem

It was a beautiful summer morning in the early 1990s. I was on routine patrol in the northern area of Prince George's County. My early morning coffee was very satisfying on this particular day. Suddenly, I heard three loud beeps over my police radio alerting me that a serious situation was about to be broadcast: "Car 851-852-850, respond priority to Lane Manor Recreation Center for a possible homicide located across the field just inside the wooded area. Car 850, do you copy?"

I arrived in the wooded area in a concrete cul-de-sac less than fifty feet from homes bordering the park. There was a completely nude female body, or should I say what was left of a female body. This incident was one of the most brutal murders I have ever seen, a revenge killing that was a very loud crime, with screams emanating through the neighborhood. Yet nobody called the police while it was happening the night before. Blood was everywhere, attracting large green flies.

The victim had been beaten, with her teeth knocked out, broken eye sockets, and a dislocated jaw. Even her fingers, arms, and legs had been broken from the perpetrator stomping on her extremities at angles on the concrete. Her legs had been forced over her head. The unknown assailant then took a four-inch-diameter tree limb and jammed the bark-encrusted stick into her vagina. The criminal used a sexual motion with the stick to violently withdraw her internal organs, spilling this gruesome gook onto the concrete. Her face was frozen in absolute horror and agony.

A concerned citizen who was walking her dog found the deceased woman. This area was not a normal place to walk a pet. We believe she went to this area to see what the screams had been about. While she did not call the police as it was occurring, curiosity must have drawn her there, and she discovered the ugly consequences of not becoming involved.

The scene was extremely nasty, with more flies and insects being drawn to the body with every minute that passed. By the time homicide detectives arrived, the stench was beginning to permeate our clothes. All we wanted to do was get out of there.

The murderer was found after a lengthy investigation. He was already in jail in Washington, DC. A detainer was filed so that when he was released from the DC jail, he would be transferred directly to Prince George's County to face charges of murder.

Murders and suicides are prevalent within the park system. Even policemen have been found dead in the parks. Many of these scenes are very brutal and disgusting. Suicide by hanging can be particularly shocking. When not found right away, their necks can stretch from the weight of their body, at times allowing the body to become almost prone on the ground while still attached to the head, looking like a weird type of giraffe. It just doesn't look real, but it is.

Murders have included women who have had their throats cut after being raped. As brutal as it sounds, it is true. These women may be walking or jogging in isolated areas, believing they are safe from harm. One lady, after having her throat cut by a very rusty knife, broke free of her attacker, running about a hundred feet before collapsing. Adrenaline allowed her to break free and run before dying.

One summer while on a midnight shift, I was driving my cruiser on an isolated road toward the rear of the Enterprise Golf Course. I ran over an unknown substance on the roadway and could hear the sound of the sticky substance spraying from my tires. When I shined my spotlight onto the roadway, I could see a large amount of blood and internal organs laying there. I was stunned by what I was seeing and called for emergency services to respond to my location. We began looking along the roadway for what was left of a body, placing flares and closing the road to all traffic.

When emergency services arrived, they brought large lights to illuminate the area. Even more internal organs were discovered scattered throughout the area and all along the roadway, creating a nightmare for first responders. Flies and huge numbers of insects were gathering among the organs, adding to the vile mix. Some personnel began vomiting and requested oxygen to cope with the disgusting odor. Crime scene investigators began collecting evidence to determine if the remains were human. Photographs were taken, and it was discovered the internal organs were from cattle. The roadway had to be washed down by the fire department when the investigation was completed.

In Cheverly, Maryland, I had a habit of stopping and looking over bridges that were above creeks or rivers. I always checked under bridges located in isolated areas, especially where bodies had been found before, such as Governors Bridge Road.

On one of these stops, I saw an unusual item floating and swaying in the shallow water. I followed this long item with my eyes and could see that it was an internal organ floating eerily near the middle of the fast-flowing creek. I called the Cheverly Town Police and requested they respond to my location. On their arrival, I pointed out the wavering internal organ to them. We walked several hundred feet upstream along the creek bank and found a decomposing body. The scene was turned over to the Cheverly Town Police and the Prince George's County Police Homicide Unit for further investigation.

Police officers are not immune from suffering mentally and physically. They are humans with feelings just like anyone else. Seeing blood and gore almost daily will affect you no matter how much you think it will not. Homicide detectives can only stay in their positions for so long. They will suffer long-term effects of seeing and handling the brutality.

I once responded to a domestic dispute involving a cutting as the backup officer for the beat car. Upon entering a residence in Palmer Park, Maryland, I saw a Black male lying facedown in the living room in a large pool of blood. A female of large proportion was yelling, "Get up, you nigga! Stop playin'. You ain't dead."

I said, "He is dead."

She continued, "Tell that nigga to get up. I only cut him a little bit. I've cut him before to teach his ass a lesson." She had used a stainless-steel knife with a twelve-inch blade, similar to a hunting knife of hardened steel, to stab the man. She reached over his left shoulder and stabbed him with such force the blade nearly passed entirely through his small frame. She then drew the knife up and over his shoulder, slicing through his bone like butter, splitting his chest open like a peach. This action killed him instantly.

The scene was brutal with large amounts of blood. She yelled, "He ain't dead! He just playin'. Tell him to get up" over and over again. She was making an ugly scene even uglier by drawing the people from the surrounding neighborhood. These people believed we as police were being unjust to this very big woman. She required two sets of cuffs to effectively restrain her, and we had to call for further assistance for crowd control. The victim, a Black male, was of small stature, only 5'2", and he weighed around 120 pounds. The woman, at 6' tall and weighing close to 300 pounds, towered over him. He would fight with her by trying to beat her with his boxing skills, but he could not fend off the knife attack.

I worked as a deputy sheriff assigned to the domestic violence unit. Three other deputies and I worked with a female sergeant. She was very unreasonable, hard to talk to, and could not hold a conversation without becoming hostile. She would lose her temper and yell, drawing the attention of other supervisors. She would explain to superiors that she was dealing with a bunch of idiots, speaking loudly so everyone could hear these tirades. We began complaining to our lieutenant, but he chose to ignore this issue.

One day in late October, my unit was given what we believed would be an easy emergency psychiatric evaluation (EPS). Two ladies contacted our sergeant and explained that their brother, who was residing with them, was very violent. He was throwing items and threatening them with bodily harm. The sergeant did not inform us about the entire situation we might face. She just gave us the address and ordered us to follow her.

It was a very cool day as we approached the brand-new townhouse. We knocked on the door, and two older soaking-wet ladies answered the door. We entered the residence, and the whole house was dripping wet, including the brand-new furniture,. carpet, ceilings…everything. We were stunned by the amount of damage.

I asked them, "What happened?"

They told me they had an argument with their brother, who wanted them to turn up the heat in the house. They had refused to do so, and he said, "I will show you."

He went upstairs to his bedroom, built a campfire in the middle of the floor, and then lit it. The fire and smoke set off the automatic sprinkler system throughout the house.

We asked, "Where is he now?" and were told he was upstairs in his room. We went upstairs to the left and squished our way toward his room. Once we reached the doorway and I peeked through, I could see the campfire still steaming.

I was startled by him looking back at me, shouting, "FBI. You are under arrest." All of us entered the room and attempted to arrest him. He began fighting us with an ink pen he was holding in his right hand. I attempted to grab the pen, and he stabbed me in my right hand, between my thumb and index finger. He sank the pen about half an inch in. As blood gushed out of the wound, I began yelling that he stabbed me. All I could see was him going upside down and being slammed onto the wet floor. He was finally under control and placed in cuffs. Instead of helping us with this idiot, my sergeant was downstairs with the two women. As I descended the stairs, I was trying to stop the bleeding from my hand. I was only adding my blood to the rest of the mess in the house.

I then went to the hospital, where I was examined. I had the wound cleaned and my hand wrapped in bandages. Since I am right-handed, I could not access my handgun or defend myself, and my lieutenant ordered me to go home.

The female sergeant intervened, saying, "No, he is staying here." The lieutenant overruled her and sent me home. As I was leaving, she was still arguing with him.

The sergeant finally retired and moved to Delaware. One day, I had an encounter with her at a Happy Harry drugstore there. She told me she was having domestic problems with her husband. Not long after, she met with her husband at the rear of a business complex in Sussex County, Delaware. While sitting in her car, he placed a handgun to her head and pulled the trigger, blowing her brains out. He then turned the gun on himself and shot his brains out too. As with most families, there are things unknown and untold that can drive a person to insanity.

The brutality of murder extends to the living, who suffer from watching these scenes even though they are just spectators. Crime scenes are not pretty or glamorous. Television shows portray unrealistic, sterile, insect-free scenes, not animals dragging off sections of cadavers. These scenes are not alluring in any sense, what with bloodborne pathogens floating around. Homicide detectives put Vicks VapoRub up their noses to blunt the smell of rotting meat, vomit, and human excrement. The longer a cadaver is not found, the more rotten it becomes. Finally, only bones, DNA, and teeth remain for identification.

I feel for the police officers who arrived on that extremely gory scene in Delaware. They, too, suffered from PTSD. The fresher a bloody scene, the more intense the tinny, copper, metal smell of the blood. The smells and sights, including brain matter and outright gore, create memories those officers will never forget.

When I was in isolated wooded areas, it was unusual to see big green flies around. If I did see them, it was likely something nearby was dead and attracting them to the area. The flies are a telltale sign that something is amiss, and the area needs to be searched. Follow the flies to the location where they gather in the largest numbers. Most likely, there will be something dead there, flowing with feeding maggots.

The first drowning I ever witnessed was at the Bladensburg Marina located near Peace Cross in Bladensburg, Maryland. As a new officer, I was instructed on proper procedures to follow for recovery of the victim. The drowning victim was providing his two children a thrill on a five-foot boat with a small engine. They were embarking on a fishing trip in the marina, where the water was very rough and at high levels due to recent rain. He provided his children with life vests but did not wear one himself. As he maneuvered his boat into the marina, he decided to give his kids a thrill. While standing up, he gave full throttle to the little engine, which backfired on him. Instead of the boat rearing up, it did a nosedive, throwing him from the boat into the rough water, from which he never surfaced. His frightened kids were screaming and crying. A citizen on the shore finally heard their plight and notified the police.

Rescue efforts were minimal due to the rough water. I was ordered to watch this area over the next few days to wait for his body to surface from decomposition gases. The gases would inflate the carcass, causing it to rise to the surface of the water. On the fourth day, his body was found between two piers. It was placed on one of these piers, and the recovery of valuable items began, including rings, watches, wallets, etc. When removing the rings, large amounts of skin and water-soaked meat were taken with it. This voluminous mix was placed in a clear plastic bag without being washed off. The removal of his watch took even more meat, which was added to the evidence bag. Removal of his necklace did even more damage to the cadaver, increasing the ghastly contents of the plastic bag. His condition was horrible. He looked like a gigantic frog about to croak.

When his family received the notification he had been found, they traveled to our headquarters to recover his possessions. I cannot begin to communicate the suffering of the poor lady as she received the disgusting bag of jewelry and meat. She was hugging it, kissing it, and cherishing it like it was alive, stroking the bag as though it had feelings. I was truly touched by her personal grief.

Once decomposition begins, gases fill the cavity of the cadaver, allowing it to rise to the surface. Once these gases disperse, the body will sink, sometimes never resurfacing. We recovered one such drowning victim who had fallen into the Potomac River near Fort Washington. He was found in the Occoquan Virginia Reservoir, meaning that after he fell in, he stayed alive, struggling almost to the Virginia side of the river before succumbing to exhaustion.

Early one morning at around two, I responded to a call to assist another officer with an unconscious person in a vehicle within a park located on Temple Hills Road. On my arrival, this person was barely alive. Emergency services had already been requested, and upon their arrival, he was transported to Southern Maryland Hospital. I remained with the vehicle to try and discover what this person may have ingested. He had been drinking a green-colored substance from a Styrofoam cup. I smelled it and then compared it to the contents of an antifreeze container. They were one and the same. He had been drinking antifreeze. On informing the hospital of this, they began anti-poisoning treatment. This person survived but likely wished he had not due to his liver being partially dissolved.

On another occasion, a person was discovered in his pickup truck with a hose extending from the tailpipe into the driver-side window. Of course, he was deceased. What was unusual about it, though, was he was staring with wide-open eyes at something outside of the windshield in front of his truck, as if he was seeing something very unusual. This stare provoked us as police to investigate whether he might have been forced to stay in the truck and eventually die. He saw something outside of his truck, but we never found any-thing connected to his death other than carbon monoxide poisoning. Sometimes people see what is called a wraith, which is a spectral fig-ure of a person supposedly seen as a premonition of death. Based on his look, I believe that was what he saw. When people inhale carbon monoxide, their cells are robbed of much-needed oxygen, causing their skin to appear flushed or a cherry red color. If they are found in time to reverse the process, they will be in excruciating pain as the cells scream for oxygen. It is not a pleasant process. On the other side of the coin, it is an unpainful death chosen by people not wanting to suffer.

We have had numerous attempted suicides by hanging. Most have succeeded, but one in particular stands out. This person tied a stretchy nylon cord of about fifteen feet around his neck and jumped from a footbridge, which was twenty feet high. The cord stretched from his weight, and he landed on his feet on the gravel bed of a creek. He was seen running around trying to remove this cord, which was embedded in his neck. Emergency services arrived, cut the cord, and saved his life, just barely.

The True Criminal

Oxon Run Recreation Center
2300 Oxon Run Drive
Hillcrest Heights, Maryland

The account that follows is the story of a criminal doing his sexual worst to a child. He was caught in the act and attempted to murder me to cover his tracks.

In late December 1977, I was on routine patrol working the evening shift when I entered the Oxon Run Recreation Center. It was here that I confronted a criminal doing the worst he possibly could to a child, other than murder.

Around 7:00 p.m., I saw a station wagon parked illegally in the rear of the park's turnaround area. As I approached, a large man exited the rear of the car dressed in a white muscleman T-shirt with unfastened pants. He was sweating profusely with a large erection protruding from his pants. He asked me in an excited voice, "What do you want?"

I explained he was in the park after dark, which signs at the entrance advised was closed, and I needed to see his license and registration. He told me they were under the seat and that he would get them for me.

I walked to the rear of his vehicle and peered into the window with illumination from my flashlight. I saw an open jar of Vaseline with finger marks in it and a blanket with what appeared to be feces in liquid form on it. I then saw a small naked body. At first, I thought it was a small woman, but then I realized it was a little boy. I withdrew my handgun while spinning around, aiming my weapon directly at the man's forehead while he still had his hand under the seat. I could clearly see his hand clasping the handle of a large machete-type knife. I ordered him to drop the weapon and remove his hand from under the seat. At first, he refused, not saying anything but not complying either. I cocked the hammer back on my .38 caliber handgun, making the distinct noise of a cocking gun. He hesitated. I again ordered him to drop the knife. He looked at the gun and then stared into my eyes.

I repeated, "You have three seconds to comply, or I will blow your brains out. One, two…"

Then he yelled, "Okay, Officer!"

I shouted, "Keep your fingers spread, your hands empty, and lie on your stomach!"

He cooperated, and I placed him in cuffs. I then looked under the seat and found no less than fourteen machete-type knives. He was contemplating using the knife on me while I was attending to the little boy.

After removing what turned out to be a nine-year-old boy from the nasty vehicle, I placed him in my cruiser and called for emergency services for the rape of a child. I then asked the little boy what had happened.

He said, "He [the man] would kill me if I told." I glanced over at the suspect, who was giving the little boy a very hard and threatening stare. I immediately told my backup officer to get the child out of there.

When I checked the prior record of the rapist, he was found to have a very extensive criminal history, including prior rapes, attempted murders, and felonious assaults on children. The juvenile boy had a sister who was eleven years old. This criminal was also sexually assaulting her. The mother knew these rapes were occurring, but she was terrified of the man. The mother allowed the crimes against her children to continue until my confrontation with him. The children were then removed from the home and placed under their grandmother's care. The suspect went to trial and pled guilty. He received twenty years in prison without the chance of parole.

These children had their tormentor placed in prison, which helped ease the burden of their horrible memories, giving them a chance to grow up without him. When I think back, recalling what this animal was doing to that child, I would like to have finished the count. He would never have heard, "Three." It would have made no difference to me whether this child was a boy or a girl. I would still be saving this little person from absolute horror.

The vehicle in which this crime occurred was towed to an evidence bay where a proper search was performed. During the search, three different-sized dildos, very worn from use, were collected. There were also jars of Vaseline, blankets with crusted after-sex secretions, and new and used condoms. The most disturbing discovery was blood from the forced sexual encounters with children. We wanted to burn the car.

Cross Street Park

My fellow officers and I have witnessed numerous rapes and sexual assaults. But the following story stands for its brutality. It was more than just a rape. It is a story of the violence used to achieve sexual satisfaction during a rape without caring how it hurts the victim of the crime. The act was not a rape and run. It was a felonious assault so vicious the victims were physically and mentally devastated.

One evening, I was summoned to my supervisor's office. He began explaining to Officer JJ and me about a park located at the dead end of Cross Street, which was located off Route 450 near Finns Lane in New Carrollton, Maryland. He told us there was a violent rapist in the park, and he wanted him captured. The suspect had an outstanding warrant for rape and was using the park as his base. We were provided a description of the man: Black male, six feet and seven inches, over three hundred pounds, armed with an eight-foot two-by-four board. At first, my partner and I thought our supervisor was kidding, but he assured us he was not. Officer JJ and I proceeded to the park. We had not been there five minutes when we observed a man standing on the footpath overlooking the lighted tennis court. He fit the description of the suspect down to being armed with an eight-foot two-by-four. He had another outstanding feature on his right hand; he had a crooked right middle finger from a fracture. We arrested and transported him without incident.

What Officer JJ and I did not know was what drew our supervisor's attention to the situation. Earlier that day, a citizen who was in a wheelchair approached our headquarters and asked to speak to a supervisor. The citizen was in a wheelchair because both of his feet were broken. He related the following story. A week earlier, he was in his car with his girlfriend, parked in the lot at the Cross Street Park. He was lying back in the front seat with his feet out of the passenger side window when he was suddenly struck on the bottoms of his feet by an unknown assailant. He jumped up, placed his idling car in drive, and drove away. The assailant chased after him, beating the car with the eight-foot two-by-four and breaking out the windows. The screams of his girlfriend drove his adrenaline to continue driving to the hospital. It was then he became aware there was something wrong with his feet. When they arrived at the hospital, he realized he could not walk into the emergency room. After examination, it was determined both of his feet had been crushed from the blow by the two-by-four board. He was admitted to the hospital and endured numerous surgeries to repair the damage. Today, he was finally able to come forward to tell his story to the Maryland Park Police.

One month earlier, a call came in around 2:00 a.m. for a rape in progress, occurring at the Cross Street Park in the tennis courts. When officers arrived on the scene, emergency services were requested. The female victim had been raped and was bleeding profusely from her genital area. She required hospitalization and numerous stitches. Her boyfriend was in shock and could not stop crying due to the trauma. Finally, after calming down, the story unfolded as to what had occurred.

The couple entered the park around 1:30 a.m. and were engaging in sexual intercourse on the lighted tennis courts. She was in the top position when a very large Black man pinned her down on top of her boyfriend. The assailant was carrying an eight-foot two-by-four. The assailant put the board down next to the boyfriend's head, where the boyfriend could clearly see the man's right-hand middle finger was broken and in a cast. As the attacker began to forcibly push his penis into the female, she began screaming, "It's too big! It hurts. Please, please stop." The plea was ignored, and her trapped boyfriend, now beneath two bodies, began suffocating from the weight. He was too small in stature to do anything to help her and had to endure the unbelievable act that was occurring. He started to cry. His girlfriend was screaming hysterically as she was literally being ripped open. The smell of the rancid person on her and the incredible pain being inflicted on her was nauseating, and she began vomiting on her boyfriend. The rapist was holding her in place by sheer force, fondling every crevice with his five-inch fingers and calloused hands. His hands were so incredibly large, one could cover her chest.

At this point, she was beyond being raped. She was suffering a felonious assault so powerful that she began to bleed profusely. Her boyfriend became hysterical and started yelling, "Stop!"

The rapist, so involved in the victim, told him, "Shut the fuck up or I will fuck you in the ass next, you sissy."

The assault continued for another thirty minutes, which caused her to defecate. The screams of the victims were finally heard by citizens in nearby houses, who then alerted the park police. The oncoming sirens scared off the rapist, who took the eight-foot two-by-four with him. The victims were left in a bloody heap of vomit and excrement on the tennis court.

When the park police arrived, a crime scene was established. A lookout for the suspect could not be broadcast as both victims were in shock, and both needed to be transported to the hospital. Four days later, the female was still hospitalized, and the boyfriend was still in shock, but he was able to communicate. He provided a detailed description of the suspect, including a broken middle finger on his right hand. He was asked, "Why didn't you grab his finger and hang on?"

He said, "I was too scared."

This criminal was not that bright, but he knew enough to not speak to the police and only asked for a lawyer. He was an extremely dangerous individual and deserved more than just jail time where he could brag about what he had done.

The brutality he left behind, both in the physical damage and mental destruction, has proven he is more than a menace to society. He did not care how much he mangled his victims to reach his personal climax, leaving his DNA like a calling card.

This young lady was absolutely physically and mentally devastated. She resembled a victim of a bloody car accident, with bruises everywhere and critical internal injuries. The rapist was a huge man with an extremely large penis, leaving her with uncountable stitches. She was in the hospital for over a month and would require surgeries to try to repair the damage. The doctor informed us her abdominal cavity had ruptured into her stomach area. If the rape had continued, it would have been fatal for her. She was only five feet tall and weighed less than a hundred pounds.

The park at Cross Street no longer exists. Metro Transit removed it, and the area became part of the mass transit system. The park may be gone, but the memories and visions of brutality are still living within us, always there.

The Pickle Man

In August 1970, I worked for a display company and traveled back and forth to hotels in Washington, DC. During these trips with our crews and supplies, a very disturbed individual, wanting to have sex with one of our six men, approached us as we waited at a traffic light. The man was performing sex with himself while clearly visible from his apartment window. He was bending over a chair and inserting a pickle into his rectum. We were all laughing at first until he came running down to the truck and placed his soiled hands on the driver's sleeveless arm. His body odor was disgusting. The driver became furious, attempting to exit the truck to fight him, but he then realized that was not what he wanted to do. He just ran the red light, leaving us all hysterically laughing.

The very next day, we had to travel the same route. At 8:00 a.m., this disturbed individual was at it again in his window, completely naked with a very worn pickle. We didn't stop at the light. After several weeks, we no longer saw him in the window, assuming he received mental help, as he really needed it. We did report him to the police. I am sure once they observed what he was doing in public view, it was just a matter of time.

This incident with the pickle man enlightened me about sexual problems that occur in our society. As I entered law enforcement, I attended sex crimes school, and as my career progressed, the individuals committing crimes of sexual perversion became recognizable.

One such incident that was used as a teaching tool was a study of cruelty to animals involving, of all things, chickens. The person involved was caught in the act of having sexual intercourse with them. We as students could not understand how a grown adult could have sex with a chicken. The answer was that chickens lay eggs. They have an opening, a hole for it. These perverts take advantage of that, of course killing the animal during the act.

Another crime to watch for is sexual perversion with human excrement. They play and wallow in it like dogs. One person was found dead in the bottom of an outhouse from exposure to elements of weather. He had tied a rope to the rafters of the outhouse, and once he was done playing, he attempted to climb out. The rope broke, and he was found standing in excrement, where he died in the cold weather.

We will never be able to stop the sexual problems among those who are mentally disturbed. We can only approach the problems one at a time. These types of individuals will place excrement on handrails or doorknobs and watch from a distance to observe the reactions of the victims who touch these surfaces. They are unable to wash their hands and end up wiping them on their clothes. The perverts find this activity hilarious. Juveniles throw used toilet paper wads onto the ceiling, where they stick because they are wet. They find it so funny when the wads dry and fall on you. This type of person is why we should use our elbows and feet, instead of our hands, whenever we enter and leave public restrooms. Don't touch anything whatsoever. Public restrooms are petri dishes and only to be used in emergencies. We must be vigilant in our attempts to remain sanitary.

The Suicide

Langley Park Shopping Center
Intersection of University Blvd. and New Hampshire Ave.
Hyattsville, Maryland

This is a story about a very unusual suicide. It did happen, and the man almost took several of us with him by using a straight razor. It is a sad story of despair when a person can no longer cope with his or her life and is willing to kill others to die.

In August 1974, I was working the evening shift from 3:00 p.m. to 11:00 p.m. at the Langley Park Shopping Center. I was having dinner in my cruiser while in the shopping center's parking lot. During these times, we were assigned as park policemen to the county police radio system, basically as wild cars. There were no portable radios for park police, county police, or anyone else. We shared joint jurisdiction as sworn in Prince George's County Deputy Sheriffs and assisted each other when in the area, as needed.

At around 5:00 p.m., a call was assigned to the county police beat car in Adam Sector for a disorderly at the Langley Park Shopping Center. An ambulance crew needed assistance in the barbershop. I was sitting no less than three hundred feet from the barbershop and notified the dispatcher of my assistance. When you exited a cruiser, it was acceptable to leave your microphone hanging out of the window so you could have immediate access to the radio without entering your car. It was the fastest way to get help if anything were to go awry.

When I approached the front door, two firemen were exiting the shop. As they opened the doors, wailing and loud crying could be heard. The firemen told me to get assistance as the man inside had tried to commit suicide, and it was a mess. To relay information to the dispatcher, I had to see for myself just what was happening inside. On entering the shop, I heard not only wailing but also saw the bloody footprints of the firemen who had exited the building. At the rear of the shop, there were saloon-type swinging doors, and underneath these doors, I could see large puddles of blood coagulating on the floor.

Once I walked through the swinging doors, I was standing in the blood with my cheap Corfam shoes. To my right side, lying back on an inclined barber chair was an elderly person wearing what used to be a white shirt. He also had on a white plastic-type belt, light blue pants, and white buck shoes. He had gray hair, but the most outstanding feature was that he had sliced open his forearms from the wrists to the inside elbows of both arms. He was still bleeding dark purple blood, looking like wine, from the gaping wounds.

A woman was seated to his left side, screaming and moaning continuously, not making any sense whatsoever. It seemed to me from this horrific scene that this guy should be dead. I went to him, standing in the blood which had already soaked through my shoes and socks and was beginning to soak my feet. I told him he was upsetting the lady, and we needed to go to the hospital to receive medical attention and blood transfusions. He looked at me and said, "Fuck off, you motherfucker. I'm going to lay here and die." This exchange kind of scared me, and I told him I would be right back.

As I started to squish my way back to the front door through the lake of blood, a large county officer entered, and I began explaining the situation to him. He basically brushed me aside, saying, "I have to see what is going on." Déjà vu all over again.

We both approached this guy, and once again, he told us, "Fuck off!" in a raised voice, almost screaming. In the meantime, I was looking for the straight razor he had used to cut his arms. I turned around and walked over to the small bathroom where he had initiated this action, and there, on the sink, was the razor. I wrapped it in paper towels and walked back over to the other officer and tapped him subtly, I thought. With my left hand, I handed him the razor.

The suicidal maniac saw what I did and sat up. In one motion, he grabbed the straight razor out of the officer's hand, opened it with professional precision, and began slicing his arms open again. It sounded like a ribbon being cut as he sliced right through his own arms. The fight was on. He jumped off the chair like a madman, growling in low tones, "I am going to kill you."

All three of us fell back on the floor into the lake of blood. The officer had the man's hand that was holding the razor while I had the man's free arm. This guy had incredible strength considering his age and the amount of blood he had lost. While we were slipping and sliding in this red wonderland, I noticed five volunteer firemen standing against the wall, watching us.

I yelled, "Don't just stand there! Help us!" The man was finally cuffed and basically thrown facedown onto the gurney. His hands were black from loss of blood. He then suddenly stopped struggling and was dead. I do not know where he gathered all that strength, but he did, and it was absolutely amazing.

We were covered in blood from head to toe. I had to throw away my shoes, socks, pants, shirt, hat, and all my ammunition. My leather gear was caked in blood, and I actually had to wash my handgun. My hair was so saturated with blood it was standing up in clumps. I even had blood in my ears. When I went back into service, I had to roll down all the windows to help lessen the tinny copper smell of the blood. The whole incident was mentally devastating. In today's health-conscious world, I would have been admitted to the hospital and scrubbed with iodine. Back then, I took a very, very long shower. I felt I just could not get clean. For a little while after this incident, I had a very hard time answering county police calls, until I finally realized that these officers needed help too, no matter what.

CHAPTER 13

The Cruelty

This next story is a shocking one and shows how cruel human beings can be to innocent animals and how our laws against this type of action are ignored.

Over the years, I have witnessed numerous incidents of animal cruelty and abuse, as well as bestiality. In my younger years, I worked as a carhop for the Hot Shoppes Restaurant, located at Southern Avenue and South Capitol Street in Southeast, Washington, DC. This area was considered Eastover, Maryland.

Hot Shoppes had received an order from a woman in her mid-forties. She was parked in a parking space with the microphone outside of her car. When her order was ready, I took her food to her car. As I approached the car, I couldn't see her, but I could see a grown German shepherd sitting next to her in the front seat. As I got closer, I could see her head going back and forth on this male dog's genital area. I then realized she was performing oral sex on this animal. As she lifted her head, the dog's penis was exposed in full erection. She then sat up with a big smile on her face and fur all over it. I left the food and informed my coworkers what she was doing.

We all stared out the glass windows. I was then told to go and get her payment. I didn't want to go back to the car, but I had to. I approached, and I could see she had returned to her previous activities with the dog. I presented her with the bill, and she paid, still with fur all over her face. As I began to walk away, I looked back at her. She smiled and went down on the dog again. She apparently enjoyed leaving a young teenager in shock.

The woman was outside Hot Shoppes for hours, relentlessly performing this act, as we watched what she was doing to the poor dog. We were young and did not even think of calling the police. Instead, we would not approach the car, even as she continued to ring the service button.

During my career as a Maryland Park policeman, I experienced people performing untold cruelty to animals. One such activity was pit bull dogfights. These dogs were trained to fight other dogs. A single bullet to the head disposed of them if they did not perform as expected or if they were severely injured. The dogs would have chains wrapped and tied around their necks, not only for training but to build muscles in their necks. Sometimes, the chains were too heavy, causing injury to their skeletal frames. Most of these creatures were very friendly to people, but they lost all composure around other dogs.

Cruelty is not confined to dogs. Cats were set on fire, shot, and intentionally run over. Sometimes humans are the cruelest beings that exist on this earth. Sacrificial animals can suffer punishing cruelty and unjust endings. The persons doing these things believe they can contact paranormal entities by killing animals. Other animals are used in science projects, which become nightmares for them. Laws have been enacted to protect animals, but the torture still continues.

In February 1987, I received a dispatched call to respond to the Westphalia Neighborhood Park in Upper Marlboro, Maryland, to take a report on a dead animal. I was surprised to receive a call for such a report. My thinking was *Why do I need to respond when this can be handled by animal control?*

When I arrived on the scene, it became clear why I was sent. It was not just that the animal was dead but the method of killing.

On the basketball court, two medium-sized dogs were found, each hanging on a basketball net. These dogs were tied to each net by a rope with a hangman's knot. Their muzzles were taped shut with duct tape, as were their paws. Laying on the court was an axe handle, which had been used to beat them while they were hanging. It was clear to me this was the work of a sadist. I cut the dogs down while taking before and after pictures. There were no dog tags to identify to whom they belonged. I called animal control to report to the site for the recovery of these animals. These poor dogs defecated all over the area due to their convulsions while hanging and being beaten.

After considering this a crime scene, I decided to comb the neighborhood, asking people if they'd heard or observed anything suspicious. The very first person I encountered told me a juvenile across the street had shot a dog for walking in his yard about six months ago. This piece of information caused my curiosity to spike.

I walked over to the residence where the juvenile resided. When I knocked on the door, a lady answered. I asked her if her son was home, and she stated, "Yes, and I know what this is about." She began to cry. I asked her why she was crying. She said, "I know he shot the dog." I told her to bring her son and husband to the station immediately, no excuses.

At the station, she could not stop crying. I informed her it was not about the dog that was shot but the current problem, and I presented pictures to her and her husband. All she could do was cry. I then informed her that her son needed psychiatric help before this escalated to human beings. He had no conscience, and they agreed. A juvenile petition was filed to the court system over this incident. The stipulation presented to them was for psychiatric help to be provided, and they complied.

This was a very sad situation. A thirteen-year-old juvenile thought out the entire process and then proceeded with the crime. The owners of the two dogs were never found, and it is probably better they didn't know how they died.

This story triggers another memory for me, "The Hit Men."

CHAPTER 14

The Hit Men

Glenarden Recreation Center
8615 McLain Ave.
Glenarden, Maryland

This story is about criminals doing their worst, even killing, to gain control of an illicit heroin trade.

On a clear but very hot morning in July 1982, I was on routine patrol in Glenarden, Maryland. The park at the Glenarden Recreation Center had earned a reputation as a heroin distribution point. In one week, no less than four persons possessing large amounts of heroin had been encountered there.

The following is conducted in police jargon to provide a clear understanding of how, during emergencies, police radio transmissions are halted once a Signal 13 is received. The radio system must control all emergency calls. The dispatcher will issue a 10-3 signal, meaning no transmissions except in an emergency. All cars on duty are told to not call out except when arriving on the scene. The dispatcher knows how many units are available, and if more units are needed, the dispatcher will order them from other areas. If the situation requires it, emergency notifications are made to special operations to activate specialty teams.

As I approached the park, I informed my dispatcher that I was entering the area for a security check. The dispatcher automatically punched a card showing the time and date I entered the park. I then informed the dispatcher that I saw three men kneeling and huddling, doing something on the ground. One of the men stood up. He was wearing a dark blue sweatshirt with the hood tied tightly shut around his face. He was wearing heavy jeans and boots and had yellow Playtex gloves on his hands. He was startled to see me approaching, and he turned and started to run. I then called out to dispatch for suspicious activity with three men in the park, with one running away.

A second individual stood up. He was wearing a black sweatshirt with the hood tied tightly around his face and Playtex rubber gloves. He, too, began running, leaving the third person behind. By this time, I was within twenty-five feet of third man. He was wearing a red sweatshirt with the hood tied tightly around his face and similar yellow Playtex rubber gloves. But he differed from the first two people. As he stood up to face me, he was attempting to chamber a round into a sawed-off shotgun. In his panic, he could not get the action to work. I activated my county police radio and yelled, "I have one armed with a sawed-off shotgun, running to the rear of David's Supper Club in the wooded area!"

I could hear as I rolled out of my cruiser the county police dispatcher hit the emergency alert button, sounding three loud beeps and stating, "All units, all units, Signal 13 to the rear of David's Supper Club on George Palmer Highway. All the units responding call out on the scene, G-George 10. Do you copy?" G-George 10 is the Prince George's County Police Supervisor for the Seat Pleasant district. He replied, "I am en route." The entire day work squad was headed my way, including my own units.

In the meantime, the third suspect, frustrated with his shotgun, threw it to the ground and ran into the wooded area, stopping about four hundred feet from me. He turned around as he retrieved a handgun from his waistband and just stood there, staring at me.

George 10 arrived on the scene. I pointed out the shotgun and then pointed to the suspect who was still standing there. At this time, the K-9 unit arrived and was immediately released to attack. The suspect started to run, and as he was running, he turned to confront the dog. The dog began attacking the suspect, knocking the gun out of his hand. We could now get him under control while the dog continued to attack him. George 10 activated another Signal 13, allowing the H sector of the county police to respond. (H sector is the Suitland area squad.) This action allowed us to establish roadblocks, where we succeeded in capturing the first suspect trying to make his escape.

The third suspect, who had been standing in the woods, was transported to the hospital, where he received over sixty stitches to his wounds from the dog bites. He remained defiant even while in custody. He threatened me, my family, and my property, informing me of what he was going to do. I walked over to cuff him, but due to the bandages on his arms and the extreme swelling, I couldn't do so. He was a bodybuilder before the dog brought him down a peg or two. The suspect continued to threaten me with bodily harm. I reached over, grabbed his arm, and squeezed, which caused him to yell out in pain. I asked him, "What are you going to do? I couldn't hear you over your screams?"

His response was "Nothing. Believe me, nothing." He was very quiet after that.

It was discovered later that the suspects were hit men who were in the park to establish control over the heroin trade in the area. They were going to assassinate the current head of the drug trade and take over.

The two men were convicted in court on gun charges, including possession of an illegal sawed-off shotgun. Both had numerous priors for armed robbery, felonious assault, and attempted murder. The second suspect made a clean getaway and was never captured.

CHAPTER 15

The Internal Pervert

Next, I recount a story of how police departments can become infiltrated by sexual predators, no matter what background investigations reveal or fail to reveal.

Occasionally, we find a bad officer among the ranks who uses his uniform for his own personal gain. I ran across one individual officer doing exactly that as he had access to the uniform and a police cruiser. This officer had a sexual hang-up and became known as a voyeur. I caught him one evening at Fletcher's Field in Riverdale, Maryland. He would approach parked vehicles where couples were engaging in sexual intercourse. Without being detected by the occupants, he would kneel and peer into their windows while masturbating.

It was here at Fletcher's Field, after dark, that I approached a parked vehicle. I turned on the high-intensity overhead lights on my car and pointed the spotlight into the parked car's interior, illuminating the vehicle. As I switched on my lights, an officer appeared from the other side of the car, flailing his arms and telling me to turn my lights out. He was sweating profusely, out of breath, and the most outstanding feature of all was the erection sticking out of his pants.

I asked, "Where is your cruiser, TJ?"

He pointed to a roadway about one-tenth of a mile away and said, "It's over there."

I said, "Get out of here."

He ran back to his car. The citizens in the parked vehicle didn't know he was there. They only knew they were exposed and were trying to cover up.

Right after I left the parked car, I called TJ to meet with me. When we met, I told him in no uncertain terms, "Do not ever put me in this situation again. Do you understand?"

He said, "I'm sorry, Larry." TJ was finally terminated after a female citizen filed a formal complaint against him. He had placed her into his cruiser. He offered her a deal to not be charged for possession of alcoholic beverages if she would perform oral sex on him, and then he exposed himself to her. She was extremely upset when filing the complaint and even testified at his hearing. I could not, at the time of my incident with him, file a complaint against him. I knew his family and the hardships my action would bring on them. I just could not do it. Also, other officers would have begun looking at me warily, and I didn't want this label.

Among police officers, there is an unwritten rule: "Thou shalt not squeal." If you report a fellow officer for minor infractions or bad behavior, it will have an adverse effect on you. Others will know what you did and won't want you around. You will not be trusted for anything. They will say, "Oh, oh, here comes the squealer. Do not do anything around him [or her]."

In a separate incident, I began seeing an unmarked red Chrysler police cruiser from another agency parked at the Oxon Run Recreation Center. While conversing with the plainclothes police officer, I recognized him from another agency. It never entered my mind as to what he was really doing in this park at 3:00 a.m. While assigned to the midnight shift, I began seeing him more often in the park. On occasion, I would listen to a story about his needing a place to go just to get out of the station. Suddenly, I noticed he was not at the park anymore. When I asked another officer if he had seen him, he replied, "You will not see him anymore."

Not understanding, I asked, "Why not?"

He informed me that this officer, while wearing a yellow rain-coat, was approaching lovers who were in the park and engaging in sexual intercourse in their vehicle. He would identify himself as a police officer and order them to continue what they were doing, then begin masturbating under the raincoat. The victims were horrified by his actions as his penis was exposed. He would continue to mas-turbate until he climaxed and then leave the area. He was terminated by his agency after the victims filed a formal complaint.

These types of individuals are eventually weeded out by the acts they perform. It's not just in a sexual way, but it's because they are outright foolish in their endeavors. They believe they will not be caught, but they always are. It is just a shame that it is always after the fact. They only desire their perverted climax.

CHAPTER 16

The Spider

Louise F. Cosca Regional Park
Thrift Road
Clinton, Maryland

Some may find it odd that I would write about an arachnid, but this spider was the largest one I have ever seen. It still fascinates me when I think of how big it was. I know this area does not have a tropical climate where large insects and arachnids do exist. Although the summers can be hot and humid here, the weather in the spring and fall is more temperate. This spider was not only huge but was also fast. It was residing in the nature center, which was heated in the winter and air-conditioned in the summer. The spider's diet consisted of rats, mice, birds, and anything else it wanted. It was not a captive creature but a wild thing living on its own…and absolutely disgusting. I have seen very large insects, including Jerusalem crickets, moths as big as birds, and large brown wood spiders in the local woods in Maryland, but nothing compares to this one. It was a freak of nature.

One night in August 1987, I received an alarm call for the nature center at Cosca Regional Park. It was a silent alarm coming from inside the building. The nature center, a two-story structure with a drive-in garage area, was in a fairly isolated wooded area of the park. When I arrived, I did my usual trek around the building, looking for broken glass or kicked-in doors. The alarm was once again activated as the sensor was again detecting something moving around inside.

I looked through the glass windows at the back of the building, illuminating the interior with my flashlight, but there was nothing moving around. I opened the door with my master key and entered. The alarm was still ticking as I searched the entire first floor, where I found nothing unusual. A Prince George's County Police K-9 Unit then arrived, and the officer and his partner assisted in the search. We searched the entire first floor again and could not find anything unusual.

I then went to the basement door, opened it, and froze in my tracks. In front of us, on the wall right above the stairs, was a spider the size of a large dinner plate. The K-9 officer and I wanted nothing to do with walking by this spider to search the basement. I closed the door so the officer and I could discuss alternative plans. I suggested we shoot the spider, and he agreed. When I opened the door and took aim, I thought about how I would explain killing an arachnid with a forty-caliber handgun. There could be a gas or waterline in the wall, and shooting into it could cause disastrous results. I closed the door and tried another plan. I suggested the K-9 officer allow his dog to go down the steps and search. The other officer looked at me as if I were crazy and replied, "I'm not putting my dog down there. It [the spider] could get on him."

I then opened the door again, only to see that the spider was gone. It was then that we decided it was probably over the door's entranceway, waiting for one of us to walk in. This huge spider was what had set off the motion detector in the basement. So the alarm was cleared as an arachnid walking over the motion detector in the basement. The K-9 officer and I stood outside, talking about what had just occurred.

Nature centers have insects and other interesting creatures for children's show-and-tell activities. This spider was not from or meant to be from one of these shows. It was a wild thing that must have come in through the open garage doors during business hours. The spider was huge, and I didn't know these creatures could grow that large. I was told it was harmless to humans, although it did have fangs, poisonous or not. I am now very hesitant when I enter buildings located in wooded areas. The spider was big enough to trigger the motion detector. If it suddenly attacked someone, it might trigger a heart attack. This type of arachnid does not build a web. It's an ambush spider that runs after its prey. When I recall its size, it stood out from the wall by at least three inches. It was an extremely ugly creature with a dark brown and furry textured body, large eyes, and half-inch fangs.

This experience, with what was just a spider, provides another hidden anxiety that adds to the need for caution on the job. We not only have to be aware of the dangers of humans but of other creatures too. It just adds to the number of things that can lurk in hidden places.

I had become emboldened in my approach to the unknown. After all, I had the weapons, knowledge, and physical prowess to protect myself. This self-awareness empowered me to confront any and all situations with self-confidence. My fear was in check. I also learned years ago, before any confrontation to, if possible, perform a breathing exercise. Controlled breathing helped me think more clearly, allowing me to control any incident, no matter how stressful. It works very well: inhale three large breaths and exhale each one to a count of ten.

I now suffer from a severe anxiety disorder, which has mimicked heart attacks. I have had to take antianxiety drugs to help maintain my calm. It is frustrating to know what the cause of these extreme reactions is and still not be able to control this disorder. Most likely seeing a psychiatrist would be of tremendous benefit to me. However, it is not one incident but rather numerous experiences that threaten me. I need to write down all these events, or the stories will be lost forever.

I did carry a blessed silver religious cross, just in case. I know of several officers who actually had two silver rounds, which had been blessed by a priest, on their gun belts. I didn't go that far, but they were working permanent midnight shifts, so I can't fault them. But I did think about it.

Things that go bump in the night can be found everywhere, and working midnights in blackened-out wooded areas with no moonlight can be very dark and foreboding. I recall an incident as a Boy Scout at Cedarville State Forest, near Brandywine, Maryland. In the middle of the night, something began tearing down our large tent. I could see clearly enough that the tent was being torn and destroyed and making an eerie ripping noise. I could see the canvas move violently without anyone touching it, as it was being pulled from its rigging of tent pegs. The only problem was, there was nothing visible doing it.

There was complete havoc among the scouts as there was no light to see what was happening. The contents of our tent were scattered about. We couldn't find our flashlights, only the matches we used to start a fire. We huddled around the fire all night, sitting back-to-back for safety. Whatever it was scared the hell out of us. It had even pulled the tent pegs out of the ground. By morning, we were ready to run out of there we were still so frightened. Our Scoutmaster had no idea what happened to us. If this had been a prank by other scouts or the Scoutmaster, it was not well accepted. This event occurred in the 1950s, before night vision equipment had been invented. It was so dark we could not see anything, and neither could anyone else.

This incident did not deter us from other trips or camporees. We still had a good time. To this day, I don't know what attacked our tent, but something did. There were only seven of us on that trip, and six were in the tent. No other scouts were in the vicinity. Our canvas tent had been ripped like paper, and we did not possess the strength to tear canvas with our hands.

CHAPTER 17

The Cat

The next tales are true stories about little felines I have known. It seems they passed from this life to the next, never knowing they had died. Sometimes they come back as a warning.

When I met my second wife, she had adopted a little black cat, which she named Missy, from the American Society for the Prevention of Cruelty to Animals (ASPCA). This little cat became like a child to me. I took care of her physically and medically. She could do no wrong, and she was very entertaining. I had never really had anything in my life that showed me as much love as a pet. Missy always stared at me and would wrap her little body around my neck…so cute. Even when she was sound asleep and snoring, we would call her name in a low voice and watch her reaction. Out of a deep sleep, within three seconds, she would wake up, meow, and come to me, which was so funny. We would play with her, and she would put her teeth on me, but she never ever bit me, no matter how angry I made her.

As Missy became older, she developed kidney disease, and I had to take her to the veterinarian twice a week for fluid injections. Her little whiskers and eyebrows turned white. The poor thing suffered, and we suffered with her. The day she was suffering the most, I would wet my fingers and place them into her mouth to ease her thirst. We had to drive her to the veterinarian to end her life. We were heartbroken for weeks, but things didn't end there.

Several days after Missy's death, my wife and I were watching television in our usual positions on the sofa. On this night, while we were fully interested in what was on the TV, the third cushion began thumping like our cat was scratching herself. We both stared at the cushion in amazement. It went on for a minute or so. I finally asked, "Missy, is that you?" Of course, there was no response.

As the years went by, we never adopted another cat or any pet again. We kept on hearing meowing in the house, and for years, I played it off as outside noises. One day, I came home during the day and was sitting in the breakfast nook, quietly thinking about other things at work, when suddenly, a very loud meow occurred right in front of me, startling me. It happened again, scaring the hell out of me. I yelled, "Stop it!" I ran out of the house as fast as I could (which wasn't fast enough). Here I was, a fully uniformed deputy sheriff, running out of the house, scared by an unseen cat.

I told my wife what had happened, and she said, "I feel her come to bed at night." I then confessed to her that I was feeling her coming to bed also, but I didn't want to say anything as I did not want to scare her.

One hot summer night, I was in bed and became too warm. I let my left leg hang over the side of the bed, almost touching the floor. I began to fall back asleep when suddenly, an unknown something bit my big toe. I could feel the front teeth on my toenail. I sat up and stared at my foot, but there were no marks of any kind. I never let my leg hang over the side of the bed ever again. Missy didn't break the skin. She was just letting me know she was there. One more incident with my little cat happened, confirming to me she is here. I woke in the middle of the night, having Mother Nature call me to the bathroom. As I got out of bed, I could clearly see a see-through outline of my cat lying next to me, looking at me. I was stunned. She is still here.

To this day, and it has been over twenty-four years since she passed and was cremated, the little brown box containing her ashes sits on our fireplace mantle. Missy still comes to bed, and I greet her by asking, "Where have you been?" She stops walking for a second as if in response and then continues to her spot on the bed.

My parents had a black cat named Henry. One day, in the middle of a snowstorm, I went to their home to check on them. There was already about ten inches of snow on the ground. I went into the house, asking if they were all right and if they needed anything. I then asked, "Where is Henry?" Nobody knew where he was. I searched the entire house, calling for him. He always answered and came to me when called.

I went out the back door, continuing to call his name. I heard a faint meow emanating from the bottom of the deck staircase. I kept calling him, and he answered every time, getting louder and more excited. I found this poor little cat at the bottom of the steps in a hollow area of snow where he was trapped. The snow was very deep, and he couldn't get out. He was fifteen years old, quite aged for a cat, and he didn't have the strength to save himself. As I looked at him, I could see he was excited that he had been found. When I picked him up, he was almost frozen. He meowed all the way into the house.

I put towels in the microwave to warm them up, wrapped Henry in the warm towels, and placed him in front of the fireplace. He lay there for hours, looking back at me to make sure I was still there. I kept saying to him, "It's okay. I am here with you." The poor thing knew I had saved him. After warming up, he came to me, and I patted him for hours.

After Henry passed away, he could be heard throughout the house meowing, with quick sightings as he passed by doorways. My parents would tell me that he would come to bed, and while they were watching television, he would watch with them from his favorite spot. Several times a day, they would hear Henry going to the litter box, making noise as he bumped against the door. My parents would also find his food dish in different places other than where they had put it. Henry weighed over twenty-four pounds, so you know he liked his food. He was just going about his daily business without knowing things had changed.

My mother would tell me that she would feel him rubbing her legs, and when she looked to see what it was, there was nothing there. After my mother passed in 2010, my stepfather, Mike, began informing me he had a very vivid imagination. I became curious and asked what he was talking about. He said, "I see and hear your mother in the house, and I also hear Henry."

I asked him, "If it is scaring you, would you like to leave?"

He said, "No, I just think I am very lonely right now."

Just before Mike passed, he was admitted to Southern Maryland Hospital with severe emphysema. I was in the room with him, and he kept complaining of a cat rubbing his legs. He asked me to see if Henry was rubbing his legs. I told him there was nothing there, but he kept insisting Henry was rubbing his legs. I had to remind him that Henry was deceased. That night, Mike passed away from a heart attack.

There is an old story of people telling of a cat rubbing their legs before they passed, like a forewarning or premonition of death. Relatives listening to their loved ones speaking of the situation passed this story on to others. Cats, as pets, love you in their own way. They may come back to warn you that something is going to happen to you. Maybe they don't know they are already gone. Or maybe they are looking forward to seeing you again.

CHAPTER 18

A Knock at the Door

"A Knock at the Door" is two stories: one of a possible home invasion and one of a fatal home invasion. Home invasions are occurring at a much faster pace now, with only one drawback. More residents are arming themselves for protection from just such incidents. Both of the following situations were prevented by armed homeowners.

On a hot summer night, while relaxing at home around 10:00 p.m., I was watching television while my wife was napping on the sofa. I decided to make myself a drink. While I was in the kitchen, there was a sudden knock at the door. I peeked around the cabinet with one eye so I could see through our glass front door. There was a female with a cell phone in her hand, and I could see the apps showing on the phone. She was yelling something I could not quite understand. I approached the front door and, without opening it, asked, "What do you want?"

She came even closer to the door and continued speaking incoherently. I could clearly see she was pretending to speak on the phone and wanted me to open the door. I told my wife to call 911 and that we were about to experience a home invasion. I turned on a secondary outside light, startling the female outside. Then I saw vehicle headlights in the street. Although the vehicle itself was out of my line of sight, I could tell the engine was idling.

I proceeded to arm myself with a handgun. When the woman outside saw that I was armed, she ran toward the idling car. The headlights were immediately turned off, with the vehicle backing down the street, tires squealing, and into the dark. After the police arrived, a lookout was broadcast for a light-skinned Black female with heavy facial freckles and dark hair.

The next day, I began examining the exterior of the house. I found when I turned the secondary lights on, the light bulb between the garage doors had been unscrewed. The suspects were waiting for the front door to be opened so they could rush me. If that had happened, it would have been bloody, not just to me but to all of them. I was a handgun range instructor for over ten years, so somebody would die.

Later in the day, I spoke with neighbors and found one who had been walking his dog. He observed the suspect vehicle idling outside my residence. He said it was a Lincoln Continental, light gray in color with District of Columbia tags. He continued walking by across the street, and he saw my outside lights illuminating the outside of my house. There were two unknown males crouching by the garage doors, and one of them was unscrewing the bulb, darkening the exterior. He quickened his pace and saw them run back to the car. They turned out the lights, and with squealing tires in reverse, they fled the area at high speed.

This incident, if it had occurred across the street where an elderly couple resided, would have ended horribly. Being in their nineties and trusting people, they would have made a fatal mistake. If they didn't die at the hands of the perpetrators, they might have died from heart attacks.

One night in 2014, another knock at the door occurred, only this time, it was happening to a couple in Calvert County, Maryland. It became a fatal encounter, not for the victims but for the criminals performing their actions at the wrong address. The homeowner was armed to the teeth, and, although probably not expecting what was to happen, was still prepared for it. If you stay ready, you do not have to get ready.

On this night, the couple was home, watching television while in bed together. The knock at the door occurred around 10:10 p.m. The owner armed himself with a 380 automatic. Before he opened the door, he could see the pixelated silhouettes of two people through the glass. As the door began opening, he was forced back by an unknown male, armed with an aluminum baseball bat. The homeowner opened fire, striking the first suspect twice in the chest. As the person he had just shot stumbled out the door, the homeowner then rearmed himself with a 9mm from his foyer closet. The first suspect had collapsed in the front yard. The second person ran to a waiting car and drove away while the victim gave chase. He opened fire on the fleeing second suspect without striking that individual.

The homeowner returned to the first person, and he clearly saw this suspect was dead. He called 911, and a lookout was broadcast with a good description of the vehicle. The second suspect was captured. It was a female, who was the first person's girlfriend. She told the police how the homeowner became a target. The dead person was a repairman and was inside their house doing a job. The repairman thought the homeowner would be an easy target for a home invasion as he was smaller than the repairman. That was a fatal mistake. The owner was a retired MPDC lieutenant, trained in handling not only firearms but violent people. All the suspect had to do to prevent his own death was, while doing his job, look at the photos on the homeowner's wall. He would have known the man would be armed, and a baseball bat was not going to do it.

The female was sentenced to eight years for her participation in the home invasion. Her story was that she had to do it or face retribution from her boyfriend, instead of the victim.

This homeowner was a hero in his neighborhood. He ended the crime spree these two were committing, leaving the citizens relieved it was over.

I do not open my door for anybody unless I know they are coming, not even on Halloween. Home invasion crimes are becoming an epidemic throughout our nation. Unfortunately, these criminals are not afraid of the justice system or the police. The next story, "The Reality," tells of bad decisions made by perpetrators.

CHAPTER 19

The Reality

The next stories are true accounts of the reality of actual police work, with mostly sad endings.

Some people believe fast chases must be fun for police, but they are not. When chases occur, they can be deadly for the officers as well as innocent civilians. Most times, it is the person fleeing who is killed as a result. As officers, we have been in so many fast chases that we cannot remember them all—stolen cars, armed robberies, shootings, and shootings involving police officers. The worst chases involve people wanted for murder. Sometimes shots are fired from the suspect vehicle, causing even more danger to everyone in the vicinity. Once a shot has been fired at police, all bets are off as to who will die, but someone will. A high-speed chase is not a game and is considered a last resort. Discovering a stolen car that is occupied is not a reason to give chase, unless other factors are involved.

It used to be that after a chase, the officer's adrenaline was hyped up, and a beating of the suspect would follow. If you have ever been in a chase, then you know how you feel after it. You want to kick the ass of the perpetrator for putting you through it. It is only natural to feel this way. Restraint is a better option but is very hard to maintain. When a suspect will not give up, a fight is probably inevitable. That is when the situation becomes dangerous to the suspect(s).

I have seen numerous people who would not surrender end up mangled beyond belief. Injuries to the vehicle occupants included decapitation, broken necks, multiple fractures of all kinds, maiming, and being burned alive. Sometimes drowning occurs when the car flips over in the water and pins the occupants inside. Numerous people have wrapped their cars around trees or telephone poles, which can lead to electrocution. Some endings are particularly gruesome. In one such horrible incident, a railroad tie was dislodged and smashed through the car's windshield. It struck the driver in the upper chest, decapitating him just above the heart. The upper part of his body was pinned to the seat while the lower portion, containing the heart, was still pumping blood. Disgusting. You find yourself attempting to harden yourself to ignore the brutality, but it will catch up with you. There is only so much you can absorb before something mentally or physically goes awry.

Juveniles find it thrilling to run from the police until it backfires on them. I know of one incident where a carload of juveniles ran from officers. When they jumped out of the vehicle, one of them ran to the rear of the car. The officer who was giving chase could not stop in time to avoid hitting the suspect and ran over him. The suspect was trapped against the catalytic converter, which was extremely hot, and was fried to death. The screams were haunting.

Police officers are not immune from being hurt or killed in these chases either. Even if they survive the chase, their heart rate and blood pressure skyrocket, and their mental stability may come into question. Sometimes they suffer heart attacks and even death as a direct result of the physical and mental stress. I always tried to prevent a chase by blocking the suspect vehicle if I could. That tactic didn't t always work, but at least I tried. When it did work, I could see the suspects' faces, with eyes wide open in panic. Officers need to stay in control to function properly and with restraint. Otherwise, mistakes will happen. As stated in a previous chapter, if you can, take three deep breaths before taking any action.

When a chase ends disastrously, the officers always respond by attempting to save the people from the results of their attempts to flee. They call on emergency services and other professional entities to assist in rescue efforts. The outcome for the occupants may be negative in the end, but aid is given no matter what.

As almost everyone knows, motorcycles and their operators are nothing more than flying missiles when driven at speeds over 100 mph. When a motorcyclist commits a felony and a chase ensues, we don't know what color the person is. He or she is wearing a helmet, gloves, and heavy clothing. At 120 mph, which motorcyclists do on their own without any police provocation, they are dead meat and kill themselves.

Just before I retired, I had one last encounter with a motorcyclist. The operator was performing handstands on the front wheel of the bike while stopped at a traffic light. Since I was sitting behind him in an unmarked car, I allowed him to continue as I knew he was going to take off as soon as the light turned green. He did just that, and I followed with no lights or sirens. For two miles, he was traveling in excess of 120 mph. I didn't need to keep up with him. I just watched him.

Eventually, he caught a red light and was turning around. He saw me come up behind him and accelerated until the next turn-around. He looked back at me, and I pointed at him and said, "I am going to get you."

He accelerated even more. I knew I couldn't as he was going in excess of 100 mph. When I arrived at the next intersection, there was his smoking motorcycle lying in the middle of it. I followed his skid marks back to where his rear wheel hit the curb. Evidently, looking back to see where I was, he lost control, and he was ejected to who knew where. Infrared cameras were brought in via helicopter, but nothing was found of him. The motorcycle, with filed-down serial numbers, had been stolen from Fairfax County, Virginia. If he was a skilled rider, he could have slid with the cycle until it came to rest. I doubt it, though, as he was going too fast to control it. When the cycle hit the curb, it tumbled.

As a deputy sheriff assigned to the domestic violence unit and working midnights, I was in an unmarked cruiser traveling east on East-West Highway in Hyattsville, Maryland. I noticed a vehicle approaching the rear of my vehicle with its blinding high beams on. I moved over to the left lane, hitting my brakes to try and see who was driving the car. The driver slowed down at the same time. I tapped my brakes a little harder, and I was next to a black Fleetwood Cadillac with its window rolled up. There was part of an arm wedged between the side view mirror and the closed window. Under the vehicle was some sort of metal object that was dragging on the ground, throwing sparks violently on both sides of the car.

I then moved my cruiser to the rear of the car. I could see the paper license tag was folded over, and I couldn't read the numbers, so I called out on my radio, informing my dispatcher of my situation and location. After this, I focused my attention totally on the car. I switched on my emergency equipment, and the Cadillac began fleeing east on East-West Highway, going in excess of 100 mph. The vehicle made a right turn onto Kenilworth Avenue, sliding but maintaining control, and then made a right onto Fifty-Seventh Avenue. I knew this was a mistake, as Fifty-Seventh Avenue was a dead-end road into an apartment complex. When the driver reached the dead end, he turned his vehicle around, ramming other vehicles as he did so. His V-8 engine overpowered my V-6, pushing my car backward and pinning my cruiser against an apartment building. The Cadillac slid by me and continued out of the complex, leaving me behind. A lookout was broadcast, but he made good on his escape. A picture of his vehicle was taken by a speed camera at East-West Highway and Queens Chapel Road, and the car was traveling in excess of 83 mph.

There was a large controversy over this situation within the sheriff's department. Basically, no one believed my story until the picture came out, proving the story to be true. The picture even showed the sparks flying out from under the car. That ended the controversy once and for all. To all the skeptics, I say, "Shut up."

When I first became a policeman, we were trained to shoot people driving stolen cars. It was allowable to do this at the time, and not just for a stolen car. Anyone running from police for any reason could be shot. You didn't need a reason to pull people over for traffic violations. Driving was a privilege, not a right. Even now, driving is still a privilege. There was no rights card, and reading of a person's rights was nonexistent. As the years went by, restrictions were placed on police functions, and adjustments were made by the police. Fast-food restaurant chains such as Kentucky Fried Chicken used to provide food to police officers until the Serpico incident happened in New York City. Frank Serpico was a police officer in New York City. He had reported widespread systematic corruption in the police department, but no action was taken. He became a whistleblower, and his story was published on the front page of the *New York Times* on April 25, 1970. This incident stopped all fast-food chains from providing police officers with free food to stop police from showing favoritism in enforcing the law. But there is an exception to every rule. In low-income areas, fast food is provided free of charge to police, at times, to keep them in the restaurant.

In Cheverly, Maryland, across from the old Cheverly Theatre, at the intersection of Route 202 and Route 450, there was a small building where an Asian family established a mom-and-pop of type store right in the middle of the intersection. When I was working, I would stop in and purchase cigarettes when I used to smoke. The owners were so frightened by the neighborhood where this store was located, they would always be so glad to see me. Whatever I wanted was free—sodas, water, cigarettes, anything in the store—just to have my presence in the store. Whenever I could, I would stop by, not to purchase anything but just to check in on them. They were so scared I told them maybe they should sell and relocate. The advice was too late, as the owner was murdered in the store during an armed robbery. It was the neighborhood that killed him. It was so sad.

My friend's brother owned the Super Liquors store located in Coral Hills, Maryland, on Marlboro Pike near the Washington, DC, line. I used to ask my friend, Ritchie, "Why is he there?"

Ritchie's response was "He has a gun. He can take care of himself."

One morning at four, Ritchie called me crying, saying, "Larry, they got my brother."

I said, "Tell me what happened."

He informed me that there was an armed robbery around 8:00 p.m. Three men were confronting the clerk at the front of the store. When Ritchie's brother came out of the office to see what was going on, the robbers shot him in the chest, killing him instantly. Poor Ritchie, he could not stop crying. I had to pick out each word to make a complete sentence. I cry for my friend and his loss. These three men were never apprehended.

There was a Roy Rogers restaurant across from the US Census Bureau on Silver Hill Road in Suitland, Maryland. I would stop in there on a 3:00 p.m. to 11:00 p.m. shift to have dinner. The manager would approach me and thank me for stopping in. He was so thankful that I thought something was wrong. He said, "No, no, no. I am just glad to see you. You can have anything you want to eat, but please stay here to eat it."

I could feel his genuine fear. His restaurant was located in front of several apartment complexes in one of the worst areas of Prince George's County along Suitland Road. I stayed, had dinner, and talked with him to calm him down. I promised I would drive by on a regular basis, which I did. Was this favoritism? This man was frightened to the point of resigning his position, scared so badly he was ready to just walk away. I do not know what happened to this young man, but I am sure he left that position before it was too late.

The fear within this county is spreading due to people going rogue. It is further becoming an epidemic, which is spreading throughout the nation. Our society has become so liberal with punishment and applying restraints to police to the point that this criminal element is willing to attack officers, as they become security guards, with no respect. We as a society need to loosen the restraints on police to regain control.

Juveniles are no different. When they kill, they should, in return, be killed. Murder is an unforgivable crime, and they do not deserve a second chance. People that do not believe this have not had a serious situation caused by a juvenile. These people evidently reside in gilded cages and see the world through rose-colored glasses. These juveniles can be very vicious. What they really need is not love but a foot up their ass. On numerous occasions, juveniles have tried to take my life, my money, or anything else. Your home is your sanctuary. If they violate that sanctuary, they, too, face the possibility of the ultimate sacrifice if you are home.

Some of these juveniles are huge for their age and will try to take you physically by overpowering you with brute force. Bad parenting, family background, or other factors should not be used as an excuse for this type of behavior. Just because they are big, they want to control you, which is juvenile thinking with an out-of-control big body. It is time to stop the liberal thinking of the court systems and provide just punishment to juveniles. Let them kill one of your loved ones and watch the injustice provided to them because they are young. You, too, will begin to hate the system when their punishment is serving a mere couple of years or even less. I have no sympathy for killers, young or old. Their background should not be an excuse for murder. I, too, had a bad background, but I didn't kill anyone because of it.

Shootings have become more frequent as a result of gang members infiltrating the entire area, but not all these shootings are done by gangs. Some may be drug-related, and others are just young people with guns who want to be somebody among their peers, regardless of the consequences. This type of mentality is what fills our jails and gives these people the status they seek.

My fellow officers and I have handled so many of these shootings. Just because a person is young, even at twelve years old, they are not immune from this type of mentality. There was a twelve-year-old who attempted to take over an area to control the narcotics trade. He was found bludgeoned to death as a warning to others. He was stabbed over eighty times while being restrained by one arm. When driving through low-income areas, you can see athletic shoes tied together and thrown over power lines. This sign purportedly indicates a snitch has been taken care of in that area and is a warning to future snitches.

These incidents, along with others, have made for a very interesting life. I have had multiple broken bones and received minor stab wounds in the line of duty. The most memorable incident I experienced was early in my career while working a midnight shift in Oxon Hill, Maryland.

In September 1975, I saw two juveniles at 4:00 a.m. with heavy clothing and some type of stocking caps on their heads in the Oxon Hill Shopping Center. One other suspicious thing was the next day was the first day of school. What were they doing out at 4:00 a.m.? On approaching these two, I asked them what they were doing out this time of morning, and I requested their identification. Their response was they had attended a back-to-school party and were heading home. I again asked for ID and for them to keep their hands out of their pockets. I took the first ID and placed it on my passenger seat. I then looked back at the second juvenile and said, "Give me your ID."

He said, "You want ID, I will show you ID." He stepped back from me and reached under his jacket, retrieving a seven-inch barrel handgun. He aimed it at my face and pulled the trigger, which struck an empty chamber with a loud click. I was absolutely horrified. As I was attempting to retrieve my weapon from my holster, I could see his face. Saliva was coming out of his mouth, flying in all directions, and his facial muscles were distorted due to shock that his handgun did not discharge.

It was my turn now. He screamed, knowing this mistake had just cost him his life. I took aim and realized the first juvenile was just standing there. I slapped him to the ground, stood on his back, cocked my gun, and placed it to his head. He began crying, "Please, Officer, please don't kill me" over and over until I finally calmed down and placed him under arrest.

He provided everything I wanted to know about the other juvenile. The stocking caps were ski masks to pull down while committing armed robberies. I arrested the second suspect and retrieved the gun, a Ruger 357 with a seven-inch barrel, single shot, loaded with four rounds of .38 caliber ammunition. It would have worked, except for one critical error. He didn't know his weapon. He had loaded it like one would a Smith & Wesson, thinking the hammer would strike the first round. It was just the opposite. It struck an empty chamber, saving my life.

Threats and attempts on my life continued throughout my career. Knowing the movements of suspects with their deadly intent has made me much smarter. Still, one or more will always slip through, and you can only do your best to survive the onslaught.

CHAPTER 20

Courthouse in Upper Marlboro

Courthouse
14725 Main Street
Upper Marlboro, Maryland 20772
301-952-3655

The courthouse has lingering effects of paranormal activity due to violent incidents from its past, from the time it was built until the mid-twentieth century.

The original courthouse on Main Street was a very small red building established in 1721, and it was under British rule. There is a dungeon-type area in the cellar where prisoners were shackled to the wall while waiting for their court appearances. This type of treatment was necessary because there were no prisons or jails at the time.

From the eighteenth through twentieth centuries, convicted murderers, horse thieves, and cattle rustlers, along with many others, once convicted, were taken to the rear of the courthouse for their punishment. Here, there were gallows for hanging and a whipping post to hold these unwilling souls for lashing with what was appropriately named a cat-o'-nine-tails, or cat. If the punishment was even more severe, the convicts were hung at the gallows and, once expired, interred in the nearby paupers' graves.

The cat-o'-nine-tails, used only for flogging, was a strap made of nine tarred and knotted cords of hemp, eighteen inches or longer. The floggings caused bleeding, heavy bruising, and even broken ribs to the recipient of the beating, with the extent of injury determined by the strength of the flogger. All the victims suffered severe bleeding from the force of the knots striking bare skin. To add more to the misery, metal barbs were sometimes attached to the ends of the knots. The beatings left the victims unable to walk and barely breathing. No doctors were allotted to care for the wounded unless the victims were wealthy. The lashes were administered once every twelve seconds, in keeping with the British Military rules of punishment. The cat was never cleaned, leaving bacteria on it from previous victims, causing infections which sometimes resulted in death. This was a very cruel punishment and extremely painful. Prisoners waiting in the dungeon could hear the cries of the punished echoing throughout the old courthouse. All the blessings of holy water and salt will not calm the cries of the trapped souls remaining here.

Sometimes the whippings were performed on men for being brutal to their wives. There was no probation or continuance because there were no jails or prisons in the seventeenth and eighteenth centuries in the United States. Sentencing and punishment were carried out immediately after conviction. Once completed, the prisoners receiving the whippings were free to go.

When the cat-o'-nine-tails punishment was dished out, these dismal souls wanted nothing to do with returning to the courthouse. Knowing that what they faced, especially at night, was a punishment worse than the cat-o'-nine-tails. The death sentences were carried out, leaving the souls to haunt the dungeon where they suffered, knowing what was going to occur to them the next morning by either the cat or the gallows. The people who died here were criminals, but in those times, living was much harder than today. They still had to eat and provide for their families, even if it meant stealing. After all, they were just humans trying to survive.

During the British occupation of the American colonies, it was illegal and punishable by death to strike a British officer. Daniel Morgan, a teenager who was forced to shine British officers' boots, was harassed, spit on, and slapped around by these officers. One day, he struck back at an officer in retaliation for all the harassment and was sentenced to the usually fatal five hundred lashes by the cat-o'-nine-tails.

While the lashings were administered, British Officer Daniel had struck, stood by, and laughed every twelve seconds. Daniel finally fell unconscious, listening to the laughter as he slowly faded away. Even while unconscious, the lashing continued until all five hundred were given. Though he somehow survived, the cat left scarring that was not only physical but mental as well. Daniel Morgan eventually became a brigadier general in the American Army with a hatred of the British. The scarring he received was not forgotten, and he became vicious in retaliation, winning the Battle of Cowpens on January 17, 1781, in South Carolina. After the battle, he was forced to resign from his position due to physical ailments, no doubt from the beating he received years earlier.

The hangman's noose used at the gallows was a very strong rope, usually made of hemp. The thirteen coils were utilized in the United States only. European knots were different. When they placed the noose around the prisoner's head and neck, it was fitted under the left side of the jaw, in front of the ear to allow for a quick snap, breaking the vertebrae for instantaneous death. To punish a person even more cruelly, the noose would be fitted behind the ear and under the jaw. This configuration brought on a much slower death, resulting in an actual gagging process with jerking and convulsing bodily movements.

An animal oil known as tallow would be used on the knot to make it slippery, which allowed the noose to be tightened or loosened quickly. Either way, the hanging was a brutal execution. Hemp rope was very coarse, which created friction on the skin. It was also very thick to withstand a large amount of weight for heavier people. The executioner would wrap his arms around the victim's tied legs, pulling down with enough force to tighten the rope and ensure death.

The dungeon at the courthouse is known for the sound of rattling chains, moans, groans, and crying. The prisoners chained here knew the next day could be their last day on earth. This thought, along with the sounds of something else with them in their cells, drove some to the point of insanity. The chains that held them were the same chains that had held numerous people before them. They occupied the same space, in total darkness. The smells of rancid rotting meat and human excrement surrounded them. The wretched prisoners were forced to relieve themselves in their pants and had only foul water to drink when provided by caretakers during daylight hours.

The floggings performed here could be heard throughout the town of Upper Marlboro, including at Darnall's Chance plantation. While these beatings were conducted, slaves and masters alike would stop working and listen to the screams. When the screams stopped, it meant the man was unconscious or dead, but the flogging continued until the full number of lashings was carried out. It was a very sobering experience to hear. The sound of a lash meeting flesh was a sound you would never forget, as were the screams as the tarred hemp and barbs tore away flesh.

The punishments of the hangman's noose or the cat were the only sources of discipline during those times. Utilizing this type of cruelty was deemed necessary to control the criminal element.

The sentences carried out here were an accepted practice for centuries, until the twentieth century developed a justice system with a conscience to stop this cruel and unusual punishment. The whippings and hangings, if carried out today, would be a crime of cruelty and have thankfully ended. The men hung here have left behind remnants of the crimes committed on them with the hauntings in the courthouse.

When the newer courthouse was in its planning stages, the gallows and whipping post, along with the numerous paupers' graves, ended up being located where the new building was going to be constructed. The graves had to be exhumed, with the remains moved elsewhere. I don't know what remained to be exhumed. After all, the prisoners were buried in pine boxes in moist ground in a flood zone. I hope care was given while disturbing these graves, including religious rights to calm their souls.

When I became a Prince George's County deputy sheriff, I routinely patrolled the interior of the courthouse at night. The Office of the Clerk of the Court was located on the right-hand side. It is here, as the sun disappears and darkness begins to envelop the courthouse, where things begin to happen that will chill you to the bone. There were broken slide-down steel security doors over the counter, which only closed halfway. At 5:00 p.m., the office closes, lights are turned off, and employees go home.

As the sun sets, the office becomes pitch-black, and subtle noises begin. As it gets darker, the noises become louder and louder to the point it sounds as if items are being slammed or thrown. I would illuminate the area with my flashlight, expecting to see someone or something responsible for the commotion. Once my flashlight came on, the noises stopped. As soon as I turned off the light, they would start again. Nothing was disturbed, with the stacks of files remaining in place. When I went into the office to search for the source of the sounds, I would turn on the office light, and nothing would be out of place. As soon as I turned off the light, things would begin slamming again, scaring the hell out of me. I would start clicking the light on and off quickly to try and fool it, with no luck. When it was completely dark again, I would stand there, just listening. I became unnerved as the slamming would occur right next to me, forcing me to turn the light on. I would eventually give up trying to find the source of the noises and turn the light out as I was leaving. I listened to the sounds fading in the distance as I walked away, never knowing just what they were.

Other employees of the Office of the Sheriff would report sightings and noises within the old courthouse, with some occurring in the courtrooms. One midnight shift, while they watched closed circuit television (CCT), an object was observed squiggling and squirming its way through the corridors. Before renovation of the old courthouse, where it adjoins the newer one, the old elevator would suddenly *ding* as if something was calling it to unoccupied floors. Just what the elevator was responding to was unknown. When it arrived back to the original floor for exit, nothing was on it. The doors would open and close, either dropping off its ghostly contents or picking up something unseen. One old courtroom in the old building has a mist in front of its entrance, almost like cigar smoke.

The situations I speak of occur at night in the low light of the hallways, when there is little activity to disturb whatever it is that is there. It exposes itself in the silence and darkness. Wearing soft-soled shoes or boots, I could sneak quietly through the darkened hallways and wondered just what was making the sounds. Nearly all the courtrooms were locked, but the sounds still emanated from them. Voices were heard, which almost sounded as if a consultation was taking place, but nothing was ever found. No matter how silent I was, I could not locate them. However, I would have goose bumps, with the hairs on my body standing up. As I continued to search, I felt like they knew I was there.

In 2004, the old courthouse caught fire while it was being ren-ovated. The fire destroyed the interior of the building, resulting in very costly expenses for the state. The actual cause of this fire was not determined. However, another fire at the courthouse in 2007, just before it was completed, was supposedly started by a welder's tool, costing tens of thousands of additional dollars. The fires were very suspicious and, although never connected to criminal activity, did arouse suspicion of criminal involvement.

The only way anyone can see or visit the courthouse is during business hours. It is under lock and key at night and is patrolled by Office of the Sheriff employees 24-7.

CHAPTER 21

The Premonition

This is a true story of how one deputy sheriff predicted her death to me.

When I retired from the Maryland Park Police, it was a little over three years before I applied to the Prince George's County

Office of the Sheriff and was accepted. I became a deputy in 2001. To restore my police commission, I was required to return to the Southern Maryland Police Academy, located off Route 6 in Charles County, to attend classes while in full uniform. I was required to make up over three hundred hours of training. Any longer and I would have had to attend the entire academy training again.

It was here, while attending classes off and on, that I met some fine officers from different agencies. One of the recruits attending the academy was Elizabeth Magruder. She was curious about my previous career since I was in full uniform. She respected my opinions and directions, and I tried to help the recruits in any way I could. Over the months, we became friends. I continued teaching her and others what I knew about surviving on the street. All of us graduated together and returned to our respective agencies.

Once she became a deputy, Elizabeth worked courtroom security along with me, and we spoke often. We were both required to work overtime, and I was assigned to security at the Washington Redskins games at FedEx Field. One evening, I was preparing to report to FedEx Field when I met Elizabeth carrying her blue utility uniform. I asked her, "Where are you going?"

She replied, "I have been assigned to the domestic violence unit along with Corporal James Arnaud [pronounced r-know]. I wish it were you. You know what you are doing, and I don't feel comfortable with him."

I was surprised and asked her, "What is wrong?"

She replied, "He is just too nice to people we have to arrest, and he allows them favors."

I said, "Well, he knows what he is doing. You will be okay. Just be careful and watch out for number one."

Elizabeth said, "I do not feel right, almost like I am not going to make it through tonight."

I did not know this would be our last conversation. I tried to comfort her, repeating, "Be careful" as I watched her walk away into oblivion.

Later that evening of August 29, 2002, while working at the Washington Redskins game, a call was issued for "Shots fired, officers down, signal 13" at the address of 9332 Lynmont Drive, Adelphi, Maryland. During the subsequent fog, it finally came to light, shockingly, that Elizabeth Magruder and James Arnaud had been murdered. I immediately wanted to go to her, but I could not just leave my assignment. After my overtime was finished, I proceeded to the Prince George's County Hospital, where Elizabeth had been taken. James Arnaud was pronounced dead on the scene, but Elizabeth had exhibited signs of life. However, this turned out to be false information, and she was pronounced dead at the hospital.

The next day, I was assigned to the address where the murders occurred. The crime scene investigator provided me with a tour of the scene, explaining where and how it happened. What Elizabeth said to me keeps haunting me to this day.

When we entered the house, we immediately saw where Elizabeth had fallen facedown, expiring right there on the floor. It was a sad scene to see the blood still present where the killing had occurred. The investigator then led me downstairs.

Deputies James Arnaud and Elizabeth Magruder had, in their possession, a court-ordered emergency psychiatric evaluation order (EPS), ordering James Ramiah Logan to be taken to a hospital for examination. This twenty-three-year-old convicted felon and drug dealer had priors for handgun possession and convictions and was known to the court system. His family wanted him evaluated, saying his condition was becoming worse and harder for them to deal with, and he was becoming combative.

When deputies Arnaud and Magruder informed Logan he was going with them, he became belligerent in front of his family and ran from the basement upstairs to a bedroom, closing the door behind him. The two deputies followed him, but he would not let them in. Deputy Arnaud began asking nicely for him to come out. In the meantime, Logan's father went into another room to allow the deputies to do their job. Logan began peeking out of the still closed door and was now armed with a 9mm automatic he had retrieved from under a baby's mattress in a crib. He began firing out of the door, striking Deputy Arnaud in the throat, severing his carotid artery. Logan fired again, striking Arnaud in the chest. Arnaud retreated into a nearby bedroom, choking and bleeding profusely. Magruder began to run back toward the living room pulling her handgun, as Logan fired six rounds at her, with one shot striking her in the left side of her head, killing her instantly. She fell onto her gun without getting the chance to return fire. Logan exited the room, checked Magruder to make sure she was dead, and then returned to the room where Arnaud was located. Logan shot Arnaud four more times to ensure he was dead. Logan then, with another associate downstairs, ran out of the front door with gun in hand. Then Logan's father came out of his room, saw what had happened, and called 911. The fire department, believing Magruder was still alive, transported her to a Prince George's County Hospital, where she was pronounced dead.

Logan made good on his escape with the aid of his friend and his car. They buried the gun in a wooded area inside a graveyard located near the house. The accomplice, nineteen-year-old Anthony Antmah Kromah, and Logan left the car in the cemetery. They separated, and Kromah traveled to Largo, Maryland, where he resided with Twyla James, another accomplice. Logan remained in Adelphi, hiding in a shed, and was discovered there by county police. He refused to come out when ordered to do so by the K-9 Unit. The K-9 was sent in, and Logan received numerous bites on his legs and ankles. When he was arrested, he admitted he was going to kill them. Logan was charged appropriately for murder.

Thousands of people, including law enforcement agencies from across the nation, attended the funeral services for deputies Elizabeth Magruder and James Arnaud. It was a sad occasion. I personally know that Elizabeth had a premonition of something when she spoke to me that evening. It was obvious to me something was upsetting her.

James Ramiah Logan was sentenced to life in prison for the murders. He appealed the decision and won a new trial. His only setback was that he had told the investigators that he wanted to kill them. The presiding judge found this out and provided Logan with no mercy. He was not insane when committing these murders. It was not that he was mentally unstable while the deputies tried to serve EPS. He was a criminal performing a criminal act.

As a deputy sheriff, I had the unpleasant duty to transport this criminal upstairs to the courtroom. I had to take him out of his cell, place him in cuffs, and walk him into the courtroom. While on the elevator, we were not allowed to talk to him. I did violate this order and whispered to him without moving my head, "You son of a bitch. They were friends of mine." I knew the cameras were watching, though they could not hear sound. I continued speaking to him. "You would not be here today if it had been me, you bastard."

Although I did not receive personal satisfaction over these words, I at least said something to this lowlife scum. I also knew words would not bring back Elizbeth or James, but I could not just let it go without saying something.

EPILOGUE

The incidents I experienced are what my fellow officers and I have witnessed over the years during our careers together. The current officers who have replaced us will see and hear these things I am speaking of or have already experienced these strange and odd occurrences. They, too, will have a story to tell. I am positive about that.

The residue of these occurrences will continue to exist long after our lives are over. The entity at Darnall's Chance will always be there. He cannot escape his destiny by whoever assigned him to it. This is the same diagnosis for the occultations at the Mary Surratt House. They will not escape condemnation to the repetitiveness of their actions in the afterlife.

The M-NCPPC is gaining the benefits of possessing these special properties. They are reaping the rewards of these places' popularity with the visitors who come to hear the true stories of the ghostly phenomena with historical connections to these properties.

I am truly proud to have served with the M-NCPPC Park Police and to have experienced these very odd situations. These memories, mostly great and some very scary encounters with the known and unknown, will last the rest of my life. I am sorry I cannot continue having these experiences due to my retirement. I truly miss it. I just grew old in my service.

Prince George's County Police Department

Prince George's County, Maryland

This certifies that

Larry E. Larman

has successfully completed the

Basic Training Course - Session 47

June 25, 1973 to October 19, 1973

and is awarded this diploma in recognition thereof

Commander, Training and Education Division

Chief of Police

PRINCE GEORGE'S COUNTY, MARYLAND

A Proclamation

WHEREAS, Larry E. Larman, of the Maryland National Capital Park Police, has been named "Police Officer of the Year"; and

WHEREAS, Larry E. Larman received this first annual award from the Maryland National Capital Park Police and the Fraternal Order of Police Lodge No. 30; and

WHEREAS, Larry E. Larman was singled out for this distinguished award because of his uncanny ability to ferret out potentially dangerous situations and individuals; and

WHEREAS, three cases in which he was involved, within the past year, illustrate his unusual ability to spot the wrong-doer; and

WHEREAS, in one instance, Larry E. Larman broke-up a would be armed robbery gange after spotting them in a park; in another, he confiscated heroin and a handgun and made an arrest of another suspect seen in a park; and in a third case he arrested three persons he saw drying home-grown marijuana on park benches.

NOW, THEREFORE, BE IT PROCLAIMED by the Prince George's County Council that Officer Larry E. Larman is commended for his outstanding performance which resulted in him being named "Police Officer of the Year" and that Larry E. Larman is wished the best in the future.

Richard J. Castaldi

Frank P. Casula
COUNCIL CHAIRMAN

A Proclamation

WHEREAS, established and effective law and order is essential to the survival of a civilized society, and a professional and dedicated police department is necessary to provide for the safety of our citizens; and

WHEREAS, on April 1, 1998, Police Officer IV Larry E. Larman retired from the Maryland-National Capital Park Police after twenty-five years of service; and

WHEREAS, Officer Larry Larman began his career with Maryland-National Capital Park Police on June 18, 1973, and has demonstrated accomplishments as a patrol officer with proficiency as a police motorcycle operator; and

WHEREAS, throughout his career, Officer Larman has received 34 letters of commendation, including letters from County Executives Larry Hogan and Parris Glendening, Judge C. Philip Nichols, Chiefs of Police Leslie and Rand, and numerous private citizens for his courteous and professional service to the public; and

WHEREAS, Officer Larry Larman also received a Proclamation from the Prince George's County Council and a Resolution from the Maryland-National Capital Park and Planning Commission; and

WHEREAS, in 1982, Officer Larman was awarded Officer of the Year, and a Certificate of Meritorious Service for his quick and decisive thinking in the arrests of armed robbery suspects at the Martin Luther King Community Park;

NOW, THEREFORE, I, WAYNE K. CURRY, COUNTY EXECUTIVE FOR PRINCE GEORGE'S COUNTY, do hereby commend Officer Larry E. Larman for twenty-five years of dedicated service to the citizens of Prince George's County. FURTHER, I extend best wishes for a very happy retirement.

M-NCPPC No. 83-14

R E S O L U T I O N

WHEREAS, The Fraternal Order of Police, Lodge No. 30 of The Maryland-National Capital Park and Planning Commission Police desires to recognize a park police officer in Prince George's County as The Officer of the Year for the year 1982; and

WHEREAS, The Prince George's County Committee for The Officer of the Year Award has selected Officer LARRY E. LARMAN of the Prince George's County Park Police Division to receive this award; and

WHEREAS, Officer LARMAN was selected for the award because of his actions in enabling the apprehension of two suspects even though his life was endangered by the actions of a third suspect who pointed his shotgun at Officer LARMAN and because Officer LARMAN maintained his composure under extremely stressful conditions and because Officer LARMAN on several occasions recovered substantial amounts of controlled dangerous substances,

NOW THEREFORE BE IT RESOLVED, that The Maryland-National Capital Park and Planning Commission officially commends Officer LARRY E. LARMAN for his consistent alertness, his totally professional attitude and his ability to increase the morale of the park police officers; and

BE IT FURTHER RESOLVED, that The Maryland-National Capital Park and Planning Commission is proud of the work of its Prince George's Park Police Division on which Officer LARMAN's actions reflect great credit.

*   *   *   *   *   *

This is to certify that the foregoing is a true and correct copy of a resolution adopted by The Maryland-National Capital Park and Planning Commission on motion of Commissioner Keller, seconded by Commissioner Brown, with Commissioners Brennan, Brown, Dukes, Granke, Heimann, Keller, Krahnke, and Shoch voting in favor of the motion, with Commissioners Christeller and Cumberland being absent, at its regular meeting held on Wednesday, April 13, 1983, in Riverdale, Maryland.

Thomas H. Countee, Jr.
Executive Director

BK:fdh

THE MARYLAND-NATIONAL CAPITAL PARK AND PLANNING COMMISSION

14741 Governor Oden Bowie Drive
Upper Marlboro, Maryland 20772
TDD. (301) 952-3796

Prince George's County Planning Board

PGCPB No. 98-216

RESOLUTION OF APPRECIATION
FOR
OFFICER LARRY E. LARMAN

WHEREAS OFFICER LARRY E. LARMAN ably and conscientiously served the citizens of Prince George's and Montgomery Counties for twenty-five years as a member of the Prince George's County Division of the Maryland-National Capital Park Police; and

WHEREAS, during his tenure with the Maryland-National Capital Park Police, OFFICER LARRY LARMAN gained widespread respect for his considerable accomplishments as a patrol officer and for his notable proficiency and skill as a police motorcycle operator; and

WHEREAS, in recognition of his outstanding accomplishments in the field of law enforcement, OFFICER LARRY LARMAN received thirty-four letters of commendation for professional leadership and courteous public service from private citizens, elected officials and members of the law enforcement community and judiciary, as well as several honorary proclamations and resolutions; and

WHEREAS OFFICER LARRY LARMAN was awarded a Certificate of Meritorious Service and was named Officer of the Year in 1982, for his quick and decisive action in apprehending armed robbery suspects in a community park; and

WHEREAS OFFICER LARRY LARMAN has retired from the Maryland-National Capital Park Police and will be sorely missed by his colleagues and friends at The Maryland-National Capital Park and Planning Commission.

NOW THEREFORE BE IT RESOLVED that the Prince George's County Planning Board of The Maryland-National Capital Park and Planning Commission congratulates OFFICER LARRY LARMAN on his retirement, thanks him for his long-standing commitment and dedication, and wishes him the best of health, happiness and success in the years to come.

July 16, 1998

____
Date

Elizabeth M. Hewlett, Chairman

MNC PPC
PARK
POLICE
MARYLAND-NATIONAL CAPITAL
PRINCE GEORGE'S COUNTY
DIVISION
PARK POLICE
MARYLAND
PARK POLICE
MOUNTED
UNIT
MNC PPC
SUPPORT
SERVICES
SHERIFF
MD
PRINCE
GEORGE'S
COUNTY
1696

ABOUT THE AUTHOR

Larry E. Larman is a native of the state of Maryland, where he still resides with his wife.

He joined the US Naval Reserves, serving his time in Vietnam during the 1960s. After returning home, Larry served and retired from the Maryland National Capital Park Police. He ended his law enforcement career with the Prince George's County, Maryland Office of the Sheriff, where he retired in 2006 on a medical disability.